New Libertarian Manifesto

by Samuel Edward Konkin III

Agorist Class Theory

A Left Libertarian Approach to Class Conflict Analysis

By Wally Conger

Drawing on the unfinished work of Samuel Edward Konkin III

With a foreword by Brad Spangler

New Libertarian Manifesto and Agorist Class Theory

ISBN 978-1-84728-771-7

A Grey Market Book

Edited and Published by Christopher D. Seely for Grey Market Publishing in association with lulu.com.

New Libertarian Manifesto

by Samuel Edward Konkin III

Preface to the First Edition

The basic form of new Libertarianism arose during my struggle with the Libertarian Party during its formation in 1973, and Counter-Economics was first put forward to the public at the Free Enterprise Forum in Los Angeles in February 1974.

New Libertarianism has been propagated within and without the libertarian movement and its journals, most notably New Libertarian magazine, since then. More importantly, the activism prescribed herein (especially Counter-Economics) has been practiced by the author and his closest allies since 1975. Several "anarchovillages" of New Libertarians have formed and reformed.

Just once, wouldn't you like to read a manifesto that's been practiced before it's preached? I wanted to. And I did it.

Samuel Edward Konkin III, October 1980

Preface to the Second Edition

An agorist publication ought to be judged most severely in the free marketplace. Sure enough, the first edition of New Libertarian Manifesto has been sold out and a second edition, taken up by a fresh entrepreneur looking for profit with his ideology, is with you, the reader. The market's judgment, to my pleasant surprise, is that NLM is the most successful of my many publications.

In the realm of ideas, two years is a fairly short time. Nevertheless, attacks on NLM have begun in Left-Center Libertarian publications and one such student network newsletter berated errant chapters for switching allegiance to "that flake, Konkin" only last month. Essays and articles on Counter-Economics and agorism appear in more and more non-Left (or non-agorist - yet) libertarian publications. A truly encouraging sign is the emergence of many Counter-Economic entrepreneurs in the Southern California area (and a few scattered around North America and even Europe) who embrace and distribute NLM. An agorist "industrial park" has been condensing quietly in Orange County between these two editions.

This continuing gratification is not idly enjoyed. It has inspired the author to continue the dialogue in two issues of a theoretical journal based on NLM, the writing of Counter-Economics (see footnote 3, chapter III), and the planning of a theoretical magnum opus, as Das Capital was to the Communist Manifesto, undoubtedly to be titled Agorism. As for continuing to practice what I preach and expanding on the practice, I may add to the end of the First Preface...And I'm still doing it.

Samuel Edward Konkin III, February 1983

Contents

Libertarianism v coercion. The nature of the State. Constituents of libertarianism and diversity of Movement. The State strikes back: anti-principles. Ways and not-ways to Liberty. Betrayal and response, action over all.

Consistency of ends, of means, of ends and means. Portrayal of agorist society. Restoration theory: restitution, time loss and apprehension cost; inherent advantages. Agorism defined. Objections countered.

Micro activity and macro consequences. Agorists: counter-economists with libertarian consciousness. The purpose of "Establishment" economics. Step by step backward from agorism to statism (for theoretical purposes). Black and grey markets: the unconscious agora. "Third," "Second," and "First" World Counter-Economic status and grossest examples. Counter-Economics in all fields of commerce even in North America, some exclusively counter-economic. Universality of Counter-Economics and reasons for it. Limitation of counter- economics and reasons. The role of the intelligentsia and Establishment media. Failure of counter-cultures and the key to success. Steps from statism to agorism and the risk of market protection. The fundamental principle of counter-economics. The reason for inevitable growth of agorist counter- economic sub-society.

Self-aware counter-economics enough but some burn to do more - fight or support struggle. Combativity inadequate without strategy. Phases of agorist growth decide appropriate strategy. Tactics that are always appropriate. New Libertarian Alliance as association for entrepreneuring Liberty. Libertarian creed is constraint of New Libertarian tactics. *Phase 0: Zero-Density Agorist Society.* Raise consciousness. *Phase 1: Low-Density Agorist Society.* Radical caucuses and Libertarian Left. Combat anti-principles. Anticipate crises of statism. *Phase 2: Mid-Density, Small Condensation Agorist Society.* The State to strike back but restrained by agorist contamination. NLA appears as its sustenance arrives. Accelerating revolutionary conditions. Phase *3: High- Density, Large Condensation Agorist Society.* Permanent crisis of statism. Need to crush counter-economy grows as ability wanes. Antiprinciples greatest threat. The State's final strike: Revolution. Strategy includes delaying tactics and counter-intelligence. Correct definition of (violent) Revolution. *Phase 4: Agorist Society with Statist Impurities.* Collapse of the State and simultaneous dissolution of NLA. Home!

Some tactics listed. Tactics must be discovered and applied in context. Activist = entrepreneur. Where we are not (then). Opportunity from collapse of statist Left. Opportunity from premature party sell-out. The concluding challenge. New Libertarian pledge and rousing finish: Agora, Anarchy, Action!

I. Statism: Our Condition

We are coerced by our fellow human beings. Since they have the ability to choose to do otherwise, our condition need not be thus. Coercion is immoral, inefficient and unnecessary for human life and fulfillment. Those who wish to be supine as their neighbors prey on them are free to so choose; this manifesto is for those who choose otherwise: to fight back.

To combat coercion, one must understand it. More importantly, one must understand what one is fighting for as much as what one is fighting against. Blind reaction goes in all directions negative to the source of oppression and disperses opportunity; pursuit of a common goal focuses the opponents and allows formation of coherent strategy and tactics.

Diffuse coercion is optimally handled by local, immediate self-defense. Though the market may develop larger-scale businesses for protection and restoration, random threats of violence can only be dealt with roots of mysticism and delusions planted deep in the victims' thinking, requires a grand strategy and a cataclysmic point of historical singularity: Revolution.

Such an institution of coercion, centralizing immorality, directing theft and murder, and coordinating oppression on a scale inconceivable by random criminality exists. It is the Mob of mobs, Gang of gangs, Conspiracy of conspiracies. It has murdered more people in a few recent years than all the deaths in history before that time; it has stolen in a few recent years more than all the wealth produced in history to that time; it has deluded - for its survival - more minds in a few recent years than all the irrationality of history to that time. Our Enemy, The State. [2]

In the 20th Century alone, war has murdered more than all previous deaths; taxes and inflation have stolen more than all wealth previously produced; and the political lies, propaganda, and above all, "Education" have twisted more minds than all the superstition prior; yet through all the deliberate confusion and obfuscation, the thread of reason has developed fibers of resistance to be woven into the rope of execution for the State: Libertarianism.

Where the State divides and conquers its opposition, Libertarianism unites and liberates. Where the State beclouds, Libertarianism clarifies; where the State conceals, Libertarianism uncovers; where the State pardons, Libertarianism accuses.

Libertarianism elaborates an entire philosophy from one simple premise: initiatory violence or its threat (coercion) is wrong (immoral, evil, bad, supremely impractical, etc) and is forbidden; nothing else is. [3]

Libertarianism, as developed to this point, discovered the problem and defined the solution: the State vs. the Market. The Market is the sum of all voluntary human action. [4] If one acts non-coercively, one is part of the Market. Thus did Economics become part of Libertarianism.

Libertarianism investigated the nature of man to explain his rights deriving from non-coercion. It immediately followed that man (woman, child, Martian, etc.) had an absolute right to this life and other property - and no other. Thus did Objective philosophy become part of Libertarianism.

Libertarianism asked why society was not libertarian now and found the State, its ruling class, its camouflage, and the heroic historians striving to reveal the truth. Thus did Revisionist History become part of Libertarianism.

Psychology, especially as developed by Thomas Szasz as counter-psychology, was embraced by libertarians seeking to free themselves from both state restraint and self-imprisonment.

Seeking an art form to express the horror potential of the State and extrapolate the many possibilities of liberty, Libertarianism found Science Fiction already in the field.

From the political, economic, philosophical, psychological, historical and artistic realms the partisans of liberty saw a whole, integrating their resistance with others elsewhere, and they came together as their consciousness became aware. Thus did Libertarians become a Movement. The Libertarian Movement looked around and saw the challenge: everywhere, Our Enemy, The State, from the ocean's depth past arid outposts to the lunar surface in every land, people, tribe, nation - and individual mind. Some sought immediate alliance with other opponents of the power elite to overthrow the State's present rulers. [5] Some sought immediate confrontation with the State's agents. [6] Some pursued collaboration with those in power who offered less oppression for votes. [7] And some dug in for long-term enlightenment of the populace to build and develop the Movement. [8] Everywhere, a Libertarian Alliance of activists sprang up. [9]

The State's Higher Circles were not about to yield their plunder and restore property to their victims at the first sign of opposition. The first counter- attack came from anti-principles already planted by the corrupt Intellectual Caste: Defeatism, Retreatism, Minarchy, Collaborationism, Gradualism, Monocentris and Reformism - including accepting State office to "improve" Statism! All of these anti-principles (deviations, heresies, self-destructive contradictory tenets, etc.) will be dealt with later. Worst of all is Partyarchy, the anti-concept of pursuing libertarian ends through statist means, especially political parties.

A "Libertarian" Party was the second counter-attack of the State unleashed on the fledgling Libertarians, first as a ludicrous oxymoron [10], then as an invading army. [11]

The third counter-attack was an attempt by one of the ten richest capitalists in the United States to buy the major Libertarian institutions - not just the Party - and run the movement as other plutocrats run all the other political parties in capitalist states. [12]

The degree of success those statist counter-attacks had in corrupting libertarianism led to a splintering of the Movement's "Left" and the despairing paralyzation of others. As disillusionment grew with "Libertarianism," the disillusioned sought answers to this new problem: the State within as well as the State without. How do we avoid being used by the State and its power elite? That is, they asked, how can we avoid deviations from the path of liberty when we know there is more than one? The market has many paths to production and consumption of a product, and none are perfectly predictable. So even if one tells us how to get from here (statism) to there (liberty), how do we know that's the best way?

Already some are dredging up the old strategies of movements long dead with other goals. New paths are indeed being offered - back to the State. [13]

Betrayal, inadvertent or planned, continues. It need not.

While no one can predict the sequence of steps which will unerringly achieve a free society for free-willed individuals, one can eliminate in one slash all those which will not advance Liberty, and applying the principles of the Market unwaveringly will map out a terrain to travel. There is no One Way, one straight line graph to Liberty, to be sure. But there is a family of graphs, a Space filled with lines, which will take the libertarian to his goal of the free society, and that Space can be described.

Once the goal is fixed and the paths discovered, only the Action of the individual to go from here to there remains. Above all else, this manifesto calls for that Action. [14]

Footnotes:

[1] I am indebted to Robert LeFevre for this insight, though we draw differing conclusions.

[2] Thank you, Albert J. Nock, for that phrase.

[3] Modern Libertarianism is best explained by Murray Rothbard in For A New Liberty, which, regardless how recent the edition, is always a year or more out of date. Recommending even the best writing on libertarianism is like recommending one song to explain music in all its forms.

[4] Thank you, Ludwig Von Mises.

[5] Radical Libertarian Alliance, 1968-71

[6] Student Libertarian Action Movement, 1968-72, later revived briefly as a proto- MLL.

[7] Citizens for a Restructured Republic, 1972, made up of RLA members disillusioned with revolution.

[8] Society for Individual Liberty 1969-. Also Rampart College (now defunct) and the Foundation for Economic Education and Free Enterprise Institute all who were around before the libertarian population explosion of 1969.

[9] Most importantly, the California Libertarian Alliance, 1969-73. The name is still kept alive for sponsorship of conferences and in the United Kingdom.

[10] The first "Libertarian" Party was set up by Gabriel Aguilar and Ed Butler in California in 1970, as a hollow shell to gain media access. (Aguilar, a Galambosian, was staunchly anti-political.) Even Nolan's "L"P was mocked and scorned by such as Murray Rothbard in the first year of its existence.

[11] The "Libertarian" Party which eventually organized nationally and ran John Hospers and Toni Nathan for President and Vice-President in 1972 was first organized by David and Susan Nolan in December 1971 in Colorado. D. Nolan was a Massachusetts YAFer who had broken with YAF back in 1967 and missed the 1969 climax in St. Louis. He remained conservative and minarchist right up to this first edition.

Although the Nolans were rather innocent and other early organizations and candidates often so, the debate on the "Party Question" began immediately. New Libertarian Notes attacked the "L"P concept in Spring of 1972 and ran a debate between Nolan and Konkin just before the election (NLN 15).

By the 1980 presidential campaign, the Nolans had broken with the "L"P leadership of Ed Crane and his candidate Ed Clark who ran a high-powered, high-financed, traditional vote-chasing and platform-trimming campaign.

[12] Charles G. Koch, Wichita oil billionaire, through his relatives, foundations, institutes and centers bought or set up or "bought out" the following from 1976-1979: Murray Rothbard and his Libertarian Forum; Libertarian Review (from Robert Kephart) edited by Roy. A. Childs; Students for a Libertarian Society (SLS) run by Milton Mueller; Center for Libertarian Studies (Rothbard-leaning) and Joe Peden; Inquiry edited by Williamson Evers; Cato Institute; and various Koch Funds, Foundations and Institutes. Named the "Kochtopus" in New Libertarian 1 (February, 1978), it was first attacked in print by Edith Efron in the conservative-libertarian publication Reason, along with allegations of an "anarchist" conspiracy. The Movement of the Libertarian Left cut away from Efron's anti-anarchist ravings and rushed to support her on her key revelation of the growth of monocentrism in the Movement.

In 1979, the Kochtopus took control of the National Libertarian Party at the Los Angeles convention. David Koch, Charles' brother, openly bought the VP nomination for $500,000.

[13] Murray Rothbard broke with the Kochtopus soon after the '79 LP Convention and most of his close allies were purged such as Williamson Evers of Inquiry. CLS was cut off from Koch funding. The Libertarian Forum began attacking Koch. Rothbard and young Justin Raimondo set up a new "radical" caucus of the LP (the first one, 1972-74, was run by progenitors of NLA as a recruiting tactic and to destroy the Party from within).

Although Rothbard was moved to ask "Is Sam Konkin right?" in his July 1980 speech to a RC dinner in Orange County, the RC strategy is to reform the LP using New Left and neo-Marxist tactics.

[14] I hope subsequent editions may omit this note, but in the present historical context it is vital to point out that Libertarianism is not specifically for the most "advanced" or enlightened elements in North America, perhaps typified by the young, white, highly-read computer consultant, equally feminist mate (and 1/2 children).

Only the freest market can raise the "Second" and "Third World" from grinding poverty and self-destructive superstition. Compulsory attempts to critically raise production standards and associated cultural understanding have caused backlash and regression: e.g. Iran and Afghanistan. Mostly, the State has engaged in deliberate repression of self-improvement.

Quasi-free markets, such as the free ports of Hong Kong, Singapore, and Shanghai (earlier), attracted floods of upwardly-mobile, highly motivated entrepreneurs. The incredibly highly developed black market of Burma already runs the entire economy and needs only a libertarian awareness to oust Ne Win and the Army and accelerated trade to annihilate poverty almost overnight.

Similar observations are possible about developed black markets and tolerated semi-free markets in the "Second World" of Soviet occupation such as Armenia, Georgia and the Russian counter-economy.

[15] Note to Second Edition: The above note is still, sadly enough, needed.

II. Agorism: Our Goal

The basic principle which leads a libertarian from statism to his free society is the same which the founders of libertarianism used to discover the theory itself. That principle is consistency. Thus, the consistent application of the theory of libertarianism to every action the individual libertarian takes creates the libertarian society.

Many thinkers have expressed the need for consistency between means and ends and not all were libertarians. Ironically, many statists have claimed inconsistency between laudable ends and contemptible means; yet when their true ends of greater power and oppression were understood, their means are found to be quite consistent. It is part of the statist mystique to confuse the necessity of ends-means consistency; it is thus the most crucial activity of the libertarian theorist to expose inconsistencies. Many theorists have done to admirably; but we have attempted and most failed to describe the consistent means and ends combination of libertarianism. [1]

Whether or not this manifesto is itself correct can be determined by the same principle. If consistency fails, then all within is meaningless; in fact, language is then gibberish and existence a fraud. This cannot be over-emphasized. Should an inconsistency be discovered in these pages, then the consistent reformulation is New Libertarianism, not what has been found in error. New Libertarianism (agorism) cannot be discredited without Liberty or Reality (or both) being discredited, only an incorrect formulation.

Let us begin by sighting our goal. What does a free society look like, or at least a society as free as we can hope to achieve with our present understanding? [2]

Undoubtedly the freest society yet envisioned is that of Robert LeFevre. All relations between people are voluntary exchanges - a free market. No one will injure another or trespass in any way.

Of course, a lot more than statism would have to be eliminated from individual consciousness for his society to exist. Most damaging of all to this perfectly free society is its lack of a mechanism of correction. [3] All it takes is a handful of practitioners of coercion who enjoy their ill-gotten plunder in enough company to sustain them - and freedom is dead. Even if all are living free, one "bite of the apple," one throwback, reading old history or rediscovering evil on his own, will "unfree" the perfect society.

The next-best-thing to a free society is the Libertarian society. Eternal vigilance is the price of Liberty (Thomas Jefferson) and it may be possible to have a small number of individuals in the marketplace ready to defend against sporadic aggression. Or large numbers may retain sufficient knowledge and ability to use that knowledge of basic self-defense to deter random attacks (the coercer never knowing who might be well versed in defense) and eliminate the profitability of systematic violence initiation.

Even so, there remain two problems inordinately difficult for this system of "Anarchy with spontaneous defense." First is the problem of defending those who are noticeably defenseless. This can be reduced by advanced technology to people who are quadriplegic morons (assuming that won't be solved by sufficient technology) and very young children who require constant attention anyways. Then there are those who for a brief time go defenseless and the even rarer cases of those who are overwhelmed by violence initiators wishing to test their skills against a probably weaker foe. (The last is most rare simply because of the high risk and low material return on investment.)

Those who need not - and should not - be defended are those who consciously choose not to be: pacifists. LeFevre and his disciples need never fear some Libertarian will use methods they find repugnant to defend them. (Perhaps they can wear a "dove" button for quick recognitions?)

Far more important is what to do with the violence initiator after defense. The case in which one's property is violated successfully and one is not there to protect it comes readily to mind. And finally, though actually a special case of the above is the possibility of fraud and other forms of contract violation. [4]

These cases may be settled by the primitive "shoot-out" or socially - that is, through the intervention of a third party who has no vested interest in either of the two parties to the dispute. This case is the fundamental problem of society. [5]

Any attempt to force a solution against the wishes to both parties violates Libertarian principle. So a "shoot-out" involving no risk to third parties is acceptable - but hardly profitable or efficient or even civilized (aesthetically pleasing) save to a few cultists.

The solution then requires a judge, "Fair Witness" or arbitrator. Once an arbitrator to a dispute or judge of an aggression has performed judgment and communicated the decision, enforcement may be required. (Pacifists may choose arbitration without enforcement, by the way.)

The following market system has been proposed by Rothbard, Linda and Morris Tannehill, and others; it need not be definitive and may be improved by advances in theory and technology (as this author has already done). At this stage of history, it seems optimal and is presented here as the beginning working model.

First, always leaving out these who choose not to participate, one insures oneself against aggression or theft. One can even assign a value to one's life in case of murder (or inadvertent manslaughter) which may range from the taking of the violence initiator's life to taking replaceable organs (technology willing) to restore life to the payment to a foundation to continue one's life's work. What is crucial here is that the victim assigns the value to his life, body and property before the mishap. (Exchangeable goods may simply be replaced at market rate. See below.)

A finds property missing and reports it to the insurance company IA. IA either through another division or through another division or through a separate detective agency (D) investigates. IA promptly replaces the object to A so that loss of use of good is minimized. [6] D Now may fail to discover the missing property. In that case, the loss to IA is covered by the premiums paid for the insurance. Note well that in order to keep premiums low and competitive, IA has a strong incentive to maximize retrieval of stolen or lost goods. (One could wax eloquent for volumes on the lack of such incentive for monopoly detection systems such as State police forces, and their horrendous social cost.) IF D does discover the goods, say in B's possession, and B freely returns them (perhaps induced by reward), the case is closed. Only if B claims property right in the object also claimed by A does conflict arise.

B has insurance company IB which may perform its own independent investigation and convince IA that D erred. Failing that, IA and IB are now in conflict. At this point, the standard objections to market anarchy have been brought up that the "war" between A and B has been enlarged to include large insurance companies which may have sizeable protection divisions or contracts with protection companies (PA and PB). But wherein lies the incentive for IA and IB to use violence and destroy not only its competitor's assets but surely at least some of its own? They have even less incentive in a market society long established; the companies have specialists and capital tied up in defense. Any company investigating in offense would become highly suspect and surely lose customers in a predominantly Libertarian society (which is what is under discussion).

Very cheaply and profitably, IA and IB can simply pay and arbitration company to settle the dispute, presenting their respective claims and evidence. If B has rightful claim, IA drops the case, taking its small lose (compared to war!) and has excellent incentive to improve its investigation. If A has rightful claim, the reverse is now true for IB.

Only at this point, when the matter has been fully contested, investigated and judged, and still B refuses to relinquish the stolen property, would violence occur. (B may have only been bothered so far as being notified of IB's defense on B's behalf, and B may have chosen to ignore it; no subpoena could be issued until after conviction.) But PB and IB step aside and B must now face a competent, efficient team of specialists in recovery of stolen property. Even if B is near-mad in his resistance at this point, he would probably be neutralized with minimum fuss by a market agency eager for a good public image and more customers - including B himself some day. Above all, PA must act so as not to invoke anyone else or harm other's property.

B or IB is now liable for restoration. This can be divided into three parts: restitution, time preference, and apprehension.

Restitution is the return of the original good or its market equivalent. This could be applied even to parts of the human body or the value set on one's life.

Time preference is the restitution of the time-use lose and is easily determined by the market rate of interest which IA had to pay to immediately restore A's property.

Apprehension is the sum of the cost of investigation, detection, arbitration and enforcement. Note how well the market works to give B a high incentive to restore the loot quickly to minimize apprehension cost (exactly the opposite to most statist systems) and to minimize interest accrued.

Finally, note all the built-in incentives for swift, efficient justice and restoration with a minimum of fuss and violence. Contrast this with all other systems in operation; note as well that in parts all this system has been tried successfully throughout history. Only the whole is new and exclusive to Libertarian Theory.

This model of restoration has been spelled out so specifically, even though it may be improved and developed, because it solves the only social problem involving any violence whatsoever. The rest of this Libertarian society can be best pictured by imaginative science fiction authors with a good grounding in praxeology (Mises' term for the study of human action, especially, but not only, economics.)

Some hallmarks of this society - libertarian in theory and free-market in practice, called agorist, from the Greek agora, meaning "open marketplace" - are rapid innovations in science, technology, communication, transportation, production and distribution. A complementary case can be made for rapid innovation and development in the arts and humanities to keep up with the more material progress; also, such non-material progress would be likely because of total liberty in all forms of non-violent artistic expression and ever-more rapid and complete communication of it to willing recipients. The libertarian literature extolling these benefits of freedom is already a large body and growing rapidly.

One must conclude this description of restoration theory by dealing with some of the arcane objections to it. Most of these reduce to challenges to ascribing value to violated goods or persons. Letting the impersonal market and the victim decide seems most fair to both victim and aggressor.

The latter point offense some who feel punishment is required for evil in thought; reversibility of deed is not enough for them. [7]

Though none of them has come up with a moral basis for punishment, Rothbard and David Friedman in particular argue for the economic necessity of deterrence. They argue that any percentage of apprehension less than 100% allows a small probability of success; hence, a "rational criminal" may choose to take the risk for his gain. Thus additional deterrence must be added in the form of punishment. That this also will decrease the incentive for the aggressor to turn himself in and thus lower further the rate of apprehension is not considered, or perhaps the punishment is to be escalated at ever-faster rates to beat the accelerating rate of evasion. As this is written, the lowest rate of evasion from state-defined crimes is 80%; most criminals have better than 90% chance of not being caught. This is within a punishment- rehabilitation system where no restoration occurs (the victim being further plundered by taxation to support the penal system) and the market is banished. Small wonder there is a thriving "red market" in non-State violence initiation!

Even so, this criticism of agorist restoration fails to note that there is an "entropy" factor. The potential aggressor must put the gain of the object of theft against the loss of the object plus interest plus apprehension cost. It is true that if he turns himself in immediately, the latter two are minimal - but so are the costs to the victim and insurer.

Not only is agorist restoration happily deterrent in a reciprocal relation with compliance, but the market cost of the apprehension factor allows a precise quantifiable measurement of the social cost of coercion in society. No other proposed system known to this time does that. As most libertarians have been saying, freedom works.

Nowhere in agorist restoration theory do the thoughts of the aggressor enter into the picture. The aggressor is assumed only to be a human actor and responsible for his actions. Furthermore, what business is it of anyone else what anyone thinks? What is relevant is what the aggressor does. Thought is not action; in thought, at least, anarchy remains absolute. [8]

If you sit up in shock to find I have crashed through your picture window, and then made sure everyone will continue to live, you don't particularly care if I tripped and fell through while walking by or I engaged in some act of irrational anger jumping through or even whether it was a premeditated plan to distract protectors across the street from noticing a bank heist. What you want is your window back pronto (and the mess cleared). What I think is irrelevant to your restoration. In fact, it can be easily demonstrated that even the smallest expenditure of energy on this subject is pure waste. Motivation - or suspected motivation, which is all we can know [8] - may be relevant to detection and even to prove plausibility of the aggressor's action to an arbitrator if there may be two equally probably suspects, but all that matters for justice - as a libertarian sees is - is that the victim has been restored to a condition as identical as possible to pre-harm. Let God or conscience punish "guilty thoughts." [9]

Another objection raised concerns what will be done about violence initiators who have paid their debt (to the individual, not "society"), and are "free" to try again – with greater experience. What about recidivism, so prevalent in statist society?

Of course, once one is marked as an aggressor, one will probably be watched more closely and thought of first when a similar crime is committed. And while work-camps may be used to repay restitution in a few extreme cases, most aggressors will be allowed to work in relative freedom on bond. Thus no "institutions of criminal higher learning" like prisons will be around to educate and encourage aggression.

The distinguishing characteristic of a highly efficient and accurate system of judgment and protection will be that it will occupy a negligible fraction of an individual's time, thought or money. One can then argue that we have not portrayed 99% of the agorist society at all. What about elimination of self-destruction (which Libertarianism does not deal with), space exploration and colonization, life extension, intelligence increase, interpersonal relations and aesthetic variations? All that really can and need be said is that where present-man must spend half or more of his time and energy serving or resisting the State, that time-energy (physicist definition of action) will be usable for all other aspects of self-improvement and harnessing of nature. It takes a cynical view of humanity indeed to imagine anything but a richer, happier society.

This then is a sketch of our goal and detailed picture or enlarged focus on the aspect of justice and protection. We have the "here" and the "there." Now for the path - Counter-Economics.

Footnotes:

[1] To cite the most spectacular so far:

o Murray Rothbard will use any past political strategy to further libertarianism, falling back on ever more radical ones when the previously tried ones fail. Robert LeFevre advocates a purity of thought and deed in each individual which this author and may other find inspiring. But he holds back from describing a complete strategy resulting from these personal tactics, partially due to a fear of being charged with prescribing as well as describing. This author has no such fear. LeFevre's pacifism also dilutes the attraction of his libertarian tactics, probably far more than deserved.

o Andrew J. Galambos advocates a fairly counter-economic position (see the next chapter) but positively drives away recruits by his anti-movement stance and his "secret society" organization tactic. His "primary property" deviationism, like LeFevre's pacifism, probably also detracts from the rest of his theory more than is warranted.

o Harry Brown's 'How I Found Freedom In An Unfree World' is an immensely popular guide to personal liberation. Having been influenced by Rothbard, LeFevre and Galambos, Browne fairly correctly, if superficially, maps out valid tactics for the individual to survive and prosper in a statist society. He offers no overall strategy, and his techniques would break down in an advanced counter-economic system as it nears the free society.

o A deviation with no particular spokesperson but associated largely with the Libertarian Connection is the idea of achieving freedom by outflanking the State with technology. This seems to have plausible validity in the recent case of the U.S. State deciding not to regulate the explosive-growth information industry. But if fails to take into account the ingenuity of those who will keep statism around as long as people demand it.

[2] When our understanding increases, one assumes we can achieve a freer society.

[3] In The Great Explosion, SF writer Eric Frank Russell posits a society close to that envisioned by LeFevre. The pacifist Gands did have a correction mechanism for occasionally aberrant individuals - the "Idle Jack" cases. Unfortunately, shunning would fail the moment the coercers reached a "critical number" to form a supportive, self-sustaining sub-society. That they could is obvious - they have!

[4] The Mises-Rothbard position that fraud and failure to fulfill contract (the latter may be taken care of by clauses in the contract, of course) is itself theft: of future goods. The basis of contract is the transfer of present goods (consideration here and now) for future goods (consideration there and then).

All theft is violence initiation, either the use of force to take property away involuntarily or to prevent receipt of goods or return of payment for those goods which were freely transferred by agreement.

[5] Society, as Mises points out, exists because of the advantages of division of labor. By specializing in different steps of production, individuals find total wealth produced greater than by their individual efforts.

[6] At this point we must introduce Mises' concept of time preference. Future goods are always discounted relative to present goods because of the use-time foregone. While individual values of time preference vary, those with high time-preference can borrow from those with lower time-preference since the high-preferers will pay more to the low-preferers than the value they have foregone. The point where all these transactions of time preference clear on the free market defines the basic or originary rate of interest for all loans and capital investment.

[7] Murray Rothbard takes the most moderate position here: he advocates double restoration; that is, not only must the aggressor restore the victim to prior unharmed condition (as much as possible), but must become himself a victim for an equivalent amount! Not only does this doubling seem arbitrary but nowhere does Rothbard provide a moral basis for punishment, let along a "moral calculus" (a la Bentham).

Others are far worse in demanding ever-greater plunder of the apprehended aggressor, making it probable that only the grossest fool who happened to err momentarily would ever turn himself in, and who would rather attempt to cost his pursuers dearly. Many neo-Randists would shoot a child for purloining a candy (Gary Greenberg, for instance); others have chained teenagers to their beds to work off trivial trespasses.

This is yet brushing the tip of horror. Far greater a travesty of justice is proposed by those who do not wish to restitute or even mildly punish but to rehabilitate the violence-initiator. While some of the more enlightened among the rehabilitators would accept concurrent working off of restitution debt, they would seize upon the victim's delegation of right of self-defense (the basis of all legal action) to incarcerate and brainwash the now helpless apprehended aggressor.

Not content with punishing the person, scourging the body, and perhaps even the relative mercy of cruel physical torture, rehabilitators seek the destruction of values and motivation, that is, the annihilation of the Ego. In more florid but well-deserved language they wish to devour the soul of the apprehended aggressor!

[8] Should telepathy be discovered and practically achievable, it may be at least then possible to investigate motive and intent; still the only use in an agorist system would be for mercy pleas - mercy at the further expense of the victim. This footnote is also relevant to the following paragraph which is why it is twice denoted.

[9] A good question is where did "punishment" ever get started? The concept is applicable only to slaves who have nothing else to lose but lack of pain. To the utterly worthless if any exist, and to very young children who are incapable of paying for restoration and are considered inadequately

responsible to incur debt. Of course, a primitive economy generally had far too many problems with rationality and technology to provide much trustworthy detection and measurement of value.

Still, some primitive societies such as the Irish, Icelandic and Ibo introduced systems of repayment to meliorate vengeance - and promptly evolved to quasi-anarchies.

III. Counter-Economics: Our Means

Having detailed our past and statist present and glimpsed a credible view of a far better society achievable with present understanding and technology - no change in human nature needed - we come to the critical part of the manifesto: how do we get from here to there? The answer breaks into two naturally - or maybe unnaturally. Without a State, the differentiation into micro (manipulation of an individual by himself in his environment - including the market) and the macro (manipulation of collectives) would be at best an interesting statistical exercise with some small reference to marketing agencies. Even so, a person with a highly sophisticated decency may wish to understand the social consequences of his or her acts even if they harm no other.

With a State tainting every act and befouling our minds with unearned guilt, it becomes extremely important to understand the social consequences of our acts. For example, if we fail to pay at tax and get away with it, who is hurt: us? The State? Innocents? Libertarian analysis shows us that the State is responsible for any damage to innocents it alleges the "selfish tax-evader" has incurred; and the "services" the State "provides" us are illusory. But even so, there must be more than lonely resistance cleverly concealed or "dropping out?" If a political party or revolutionary army is inappropriate and self-defeating for libertarian goals, what collective action works? The answer is agorism.

It is possible, practical, and even profitable to entrepreneur large collections of humanity from statist society to the agora. This is, in the deepest sense, true revolutionary activity and will be covered in the next chapter. But to understand this macro answer, we must first outline the micro answer. [1]

The function of the pseudo-science of Establishment economics, even more than making predictions (like the Imperial Roman augurers) for the ruling class, is to mystify and confuse the ruled class as to where their wealth is going and how it is taken. An explanation of how people keep their wealth and property from the State is then Counter-Establishment economics, or Counter- Economics [2] for short. The actual practice of human actions that evade, avoid and defy the State is counter-economic activity, but in the same sloppy way "economics" refers to both the science and what it studies, Counter- Economics will undoubtedly be used. Since this writing is Counter-Economic theory itself, what will be referred to as Counter-Economics is the practice.

Mapping and describing all or even a significantly useful part of Counter-Economics will require at least a full volume itself. [3] Just enough will be sketched here to provide understanding for the rest of the manifesto.

Going from an agorist society to a statist one should be uphill work, equivalent to a path of high negative entropy in physics. After all, once one is living in and understanding a well-run free society, why would one wish to return to systematic coercion, plunder, and anxiety? Spreading ignorance and irrationality among the knowledgeable and rational is difficult; mystifying that which is already clearly understood is nearly impossible. The agorist society should be fairly stable relative to decadence, though highly open to improvement.

Let us run backwards in time, like running a film backward, from the agorist society to the present statist society. What would we expect to see?

Pockets of statism, mostly contiguous in territory since the State requires regional monopolies, would first appear. The remaining victims are becoming more and more aware of the wonderful free world around them and "evaporating" from these pockets. Large syndicates of market protection agencies are containing the State by defending those who have signed up for protection- insurance. Most importantly, those outside the statist pockets or sub-societies are enjoying an agorist society save for a higher cost of insurance premiums and some care as to where they travel. The agorists could co-exist with statists at this point, maintaining an isolationist "foreign policy" since the costs of invasion of statist sub-societies and liberation would be higher than immediate returns (unless the State launches an all-out last aggression), but there is no real reason to imagine the remaining victims will choose to remain oppressed when the libertarian alternative is so visible and accessible. The State's areas are like a super-saturated solution ready to precipitate anarchy.

Run backward another step and we find the situation reversed. We find larger sectors of society under Statism and smaller ones living as agorically as possible. However, there is one visible difference: the agorists need not be territorially contiguous. They can live anywhere, though they will tend to associate with their fellow agorists not only for social reinforcement but for ease and profitability of trade. It's always safer and more profitable to deal with more trustworthy customers and suppliers. The tendency is for greater association among more agorist individuals and for dissociation with more statist elements. (This tendency is not only theoretically strong; it already exists in embryonic practice today.) Some easily defendable territories, perhaps in space or islands in the ocean (or under the ocean) or big-city "ghettos" may be almost entirely agorist, where the State is impotent to crush them. But most agorists will live within statist-claimed areas.

There will be a spectrum of the degree of agorism in most individuals, as there is today, with a few benefiting from the State being highly statist, a few fully conscious of the agorist alternative and competent as living free to the hilt, and the rest in the middle with varying degrees of confusion.

Finally, we step back to where only a handful understand agorism, the vast majority perceiving illusory gains from the existence of the State or unable to perceive an alternative, and the statists themselves: the government apparatus and the class defined by receiving a new gain from the State's intervention in the Market. [4]

This is a description of our present society. We are "home."

Before we reverse course and describe the path from statism to agorism, let us look around at our present society with our newly-acquired agorist perception. Much as a traveler who returns home and sees things in a new light from what he or she has learned from foreign lands and ways of life, we may gain new insights on our present circumstances.

Besides a few enlightened New Libertarians tolerated in the more liberal statist areas on the globe ("toleration" exists to the degree of libertarian contamination of statism), we now perceive something else: large numbers of people who are acting in an agorist manner with little understanding of any theory but who are induced by material gain to evade, avoid, or defy the State. Surely they are a hopeful potential?

In the Soviet Union, a bastion of arch-statism and a nearly totally collapsed "official" economy, a giant black market provides the Russians, Armenian, Ukrainian and others with everything from food to television repair to official papers and favors from the ruling class. As the Guardian Weekly reports, Burma is almost a total black market with the government reduced to an army, police, and a few strutting politicians. In varying degrees, this is true of nearly all the Second and Third Worlds.

What of the "First" World? In the social-democrat countries, the black market is smaller because the "white market" of legally accepted market transactions is larger, but the former is still quite prominent. Italy, for example, has a "problem" of a large part of its civil services which works officially from 7 A.M. to 2 P.M. working unofficially at various jobs the rest of the day earning "black" money. The Netherlands has a large black market in housing because of the high regulation of this industry. Denmark has a tax evasion movement so large that those in it seduced to politics have formed the second largest party. And these are only the grossest examples that the press has been able or willing to cover. Currency controls are evaded rampantly; in France, for example, everyone is assumed to have a large gold stash and trips to Switzerland for more than touring and skiing are commonplace.

To really appreciate the extent of this counter-economic activity, one must view the relatively free "capitalist" economies. Let us look at the black and grey markets [5] in North America and remember this is the case of lowest activity in the world today.

According to the American Internal Revenue Service, at least twenty million people belong in the "underground economy" of tax evaders using cash to avoid detections of transactions or barter exchange. Millions keep money in gold or in foreign accounts to avoid the hidden taxation of inflation. Millions of "illegal aliens" are employed, according to the Immigration and Naturalization Service. Millions more deal or consume marijuana and other proscribed drugs, including laetrile and forbidden medical material.

And there are all the practitioners of "victimless crimes." Besides drug use, there are prostitution, pornography, bootlegging, false identification papers, gambling, and proscribed sexual conduct between consenting adults. Regardless of "reform movements" to gain political acceptance of these acts, the populace has chosen to act now - and by so doing are creating a counter-economy.

It doesn't stop here. Since the 55 mph speed limit enacted federally in the U.S., most Americans have become counter-economic drivers. The trucking industry has developed CB communications to evade state enforcement of regulations. For independents who can make four runs at 75 mph rather than three runs at 55 mph, counter-economic driving is a question of survival.

The ancient custom of smuggling thrives today from boatloads of marijuana and foreign appliances with high tariffs and truckloads of people from less-developed countries to the tourists stashing a little extra in their luggage and not reporting to customs agents.

Nearly everyone engages in some sort of misrepresentation or misdirection on their tax forms, off-the-books payments for services, unreported trade with relatives and illegal sexual positions with their mates. To some extent, then, everybody is a counter-economist! And this is predictable from libertarian theory. Nearly every aspect of human action has statist legislation prohibiting, regulating or controlling it. These laws are so numerous that "Libertarian" Party which prevented any new legislation and briskly repealed ten or twenty laws a session would not have significantly repealed the State (let alone the mechanism itself!) for a millennium! [6]

Obviously, the State is unable to obtain enforcement of its edicts. Yet the State continues. And if everyone is somewhat counter-economic, why hasn't the Counter-Economy overwhelmed the economy?

Outside of North America we can add the effect of imperialism. The Soviet Union has received support from the more developed countries in the 1930's and large quantities of instruments of violence during World War II. Even today, "trade" heavily subsidized by non-repayable loans props up the Soviet and new Chinese regimes. This capital (or anti-capital, being destructive of value) flow, together with military aid, from both blocs maintains regimes in the rest of the globe. But that does not explain the North American case.

What exists everywhere on Earth allowing the State to continue is the sanction of the victim. [7] Every victim of statism has internalized the State to some degree. The IRS's annual proclamation that the income tax depends on "voluntary compliance" is ironically true. Should the taxpayers completely cut off the blood supply, the Vampire State would helplessly perish; its unpaid police and army deserting almost immediately, deranging the Monster. If everyone abandoned "legal tender" for gold and goods in contracts and other exchanges, it is doubtful that even taxation could sustain the modern State. [8]

This is where the State's control of education and the information media, either directly or through ruling-class ownership, becomes crucial. In earlier days, the established priesthood served the function to sanctify the king and aristocracy, mystify the relations of oppression, and induce guilt in evaders and resisters. The disestablishment of religion has put this burden on the new intellectual class (what the Russians called the intelligentsia). Some intellectuals, holding truth as their highest value (as did earlier dissenting theologians and clerics), do work at clarifying rather than mystifying, but they are dismissed or reviled and kept away from State and foundation-controlled income. Thus is the phenomenon of dissidence and revisionism created; and thus is the attitude of anti-intellectualism generated among the populace who suspect or incompletely understand the function of the Court Intellectual.

Note well how anarchist intellectuals are attacked and repressed under every State; and those arguing for an overthrow of the present ruling class - even only to replace it with another - are suppressed. Those who propose changes which eliminate some beneficiaries of the State and add others are often lauded by the benefiting elements of the Higher Circles and attacked by the potential losers.

A common characteristic of most hardened black marketeers is their guilt. They wish to "make their bundle" and return to the "straight society." Bootleggers and hookers all long some day for re-acceptance in society - even when they form a supportive "sub-society" of outcasts. Yet there have been exceptions to this phenomenon of longing for acceptance: the religious dissenting communities of the 1700s, the political utopian communities of the 1800s, and most recently, the counter-culture of the hippies and New Left. What they had was a conviction that their sub-society was superior to the rest of society. The fearful reaction to themselves they generated in the rest of society was the fear they were correct.

All of these examples of self-sustaining sub-societies failed for one overriding reason: ignorance of economics. No social binding, no mater how beautiful, can overcome the basic glue of society - division of labor. The anti-market commune defies the only enforceable law - the law of nature. The basic organizational structure of society (above the family) is not the commune (or tribe or extended tribe or State) but the agora. No matter how many wish communism to work and devote themselves to it, it will fail. They can hold back agorism indefinitely by great effort, but when they let go, the "flow" or "Invisible Hand" or "tides of history" or "profit incentive" or "doing what comes naturally" or "spontaneity" will carry society inexorably closer to the pure agora.

Why is there such resistance to eventual happiness? Psychologists have been dealing with that since they began their embryonic science. But we can at least give two broad answers when it comes to socioeconomic questions: internalization of antiprinciples (those seeming like principles but actually contrary to natural law) and the opposition of vested interests.

Now we can see clearly what is needed to create a libertarian society. On the one hand we need the education of the libertarian activists and the consciousness-raising of counter-economists to libertarian understanding and mutual supportiveness. "We are right, we are better, we are surviving in a moral, consistent way and we are building a better society - of benefit to ourselves and others," our counter-economic "encounter groups" might affirm.

Note well libertarian activists who are not themselves practicing counter-economists are unlikely to be convincing. "Libertarian" political candidates undercut everything they say (of value) by what they are doing; some candidates have even held jobs in taxing bureaus and defense departments!

On the other hand, we must defend ourselves against the vested interests or at the very least lower their oppression as much as possible. If we eschew reformist activity as counter-productive, how will we achieve that?

One way is to bring more and more people into the counter-economy and lower the plunder available to the State. But evasion isn't enough; how do we protect ourselves and even counter-attack?

Slowly but steadily we will move to the free society turning more counter-economists onto libertarianism and more libertarians onto counter-economics, finally integrating theory and practice. The counter-economy will grow and spread to the next step we saw in our trip backward, with an ever-larger agorist sub-society embedded in the statist society. Some agorists may even condense into discernible districts and ghettos and predominate in islands or space colonies. At this point, the question of protection and defense will become important.

Using our agorist model (Chapter 2), we can see how the protection industry must evolve. Firstly, why do people engage in counter-economics with no protection? The pay-off for the risk they take is greater than their expected loss. This statement is true, of course, for all economic activity, but for counter-economics it requires special emphasis:

The fundamental principle of counter- economics is to trade risk for profit. [9]

The higher the expected profit, the greater the risk taken. Note that if risk is lowered, a lot more would be attempted and accomplished - surely an indicator that a free society is wealthier than an un-free one.

Risk may be lowered by increasing care, precautions, security (locks and stashes), and by trusting fewer persons of higher trustworthiness. The last indicates a high preference for dealing with fellow agorist and a strong economic incentive binding an agorist sub-society and an incentive to recruit or support recruitment.

Counter-economic entrepreneurs have an incentive to provide better security devices, places of concealment, instructions to help evasion and screen potential customers and suppliers for other counter-economic entrepreneurs. And thus is the counter-economic protection industry born.

As it grows, it may begin insuring against "bursts," lowering counter-economic risks further and accelerating counter-economic growth. Then it may provide lookouts and guarded areas of safekeeping with alarm systems and highly technological concealment mechanisms. Guards may be provided against real criminals (other than the State). Already many residential, business and even minority districts have private patrols, having given up on the State's alleged protection of property.

Along the way the risk of contract-violation between counter-economic traders will be lowered by arbitration. Then the protection agencies will start providing contract enforcement between agorists, although the greatest "enforcer" in the early stages will be the State to which each can turn the other cone into. Yet that act would quickly result in one's expulsion from the sub-society; so an internal enforcement mechanism will be valued.

In the final stages counter-economist transactions with statists will be enforceable by the protection agencies and the agorists protected against the criminality of the State. [10]

At this point we have reached the final step before the achievement of a libertarian society. Society is divided between large agorist areas inviolate and statist sectors. And we stand on the brink of Revolution.

Footnotes:

[1] Micro and macro are terms from present Establishment economics. While Counter-Economics is part of agorism (until the State is gone), agorism includes both Counter-Economics in practice and libertarianism in theory. Since that theory includes an awareness of the consequences of large-scale Counter-Economic practice, I will use agorist in the macro sense and counter-economic in the micro sense. Since the division is inherently ambiguous, some overlap and interchangeability will occur.

[2] "Counter-Economics" was formed the same way as "counter-culture;" it does not mean anti-economic science any more than counter-culture was anti-culture.

[3] This volume, Counter-Economics (the book), has been begun and should be completed in 1981 and published in 1982 one way or the other, Market willing!

o Note to Second Edition: The Market is not yet willing, but soon...

[4] That class has been called the Ruling Class, Power Elite, or Conspiracy, depending on whether the analysis comes from a Marxist, Liberal, or Bircher background. The terms will be used interchangeably to show the commonality of the identification.

[5] While some coercive acts are often lumped into the label "black market," such as murder and theft, the vast majority of this "organized crime" is perfectly legitimate to a libertarian, though occasionally unsavory. The Mafia, for example, is not black market but acts as government over some of the black market which collects protection money (taxes) from its victims and enforces its control with executions and beatings (law enforcement), and even conducts wars when its monopoly is threatened. These acts will be considered red market to differentiate them from the moral acts of the black market which will be discussed below. In short, the "black market" is anything non-violent prohibited by the State and carried on anyways.

The "grey market" is used here to mean dealing in goods and services not themselves illegal but obtained or distributed in ways legislated against by The State. Much of what is called "white-collar crime" falls under this and is smiled upon by most of society.

Where one draws the line between black and grey market depends largely on the state of consciousness of the society one is in. The red market is clearly separable. Murder is red market; defending oneself against a criminal (when the State forbids self-defense) - including a police officer - is black in New York City and grey in Orange County.

[6] Thus an "L"P would perpetuate statism. In addition, and "L"P would preserve the ill-gotten gain of the ruling class and maintain the State's enforcement and execution.

[7] An example of how this works may be helpful. Suppose I wished to receive and sell contraband or evade a tax or violate a regulation. Let's say I can make $100,000 a transaction.

Using government figures on criminal apprehension, always exaggerated in the State's favor simply because they cannot know how much we got away with, I find an apprehension rate of 20%. One may then find out the percentage of those cases that come for trial and the percentage of those that result in conviction even with a good lawyer. Let's say 25% make it to trial and 50% result in conviction. (The latter is high but we'll throw in the legal fees involved so that even a decision involving loss of legal costs but acquittal is still a "loss.") I therefore incur a 2.5% risk (.20 x .25 x .50 = 0.025). This is high for most real cases.

Suppose my maximum fine is $500,000 or five years in jail - or both. Excluding my counter-economic transactions (one certainly cannot count them when deciding whether or not to do them), I might make $20,000 a year so that I would lose another $100,000. It's very hard to ascribe a value to five years of incarceration, but at least in our present society it's not too much worse than other institutionalization (school, army, hospital) and at least the counter-economist won't be plagued with guilt and remorse.

So I weigh 2.5% of $600,000 loss or $15,000 and five years against $100,000 gain! And I could easily insure myself for $14,000 (or less) to pay all costs and fines! In short, it works.

[8] It probably should be noted explicitly that businesses could grow quite large in the counter-economy. Whether or not "wage workers" would exist instead of "independent contractors" for all steps of production is arguable, but this author feels that the whole concept of "worker-boss" is a holdover from feudalism and not, as Marx claims, fundamental to "capitalism." Of course, capital-statism is the opposite of what the libertarian advocates.

Furthermore, even large businesses today could go partially counter-economic, leaving a portion in the "white market" to satisfy government agents and pay some modicum of taxes and report a token number of workers. The rest of the business would (and already often does) expand off the books with independent contractors who supply, service, and distribute the finished product. Nobody, no business, no worker, and no entrepreneur need be white market.

IV. Revolution: Our Strategy

Our condition has been analyzed, our goal perceived, the mechanism has been spelled out and a set of pathways have been mapped out. Should we simply go counter-economic ourselves, educate ourselves in libertarianism and inform others by word and deed, we shall reach our libertarian society. Indeed, this is sufficient for most people and enough to be expected. No New Libertarian should ever berate libertarian counter-economists for not doing more. They are agorists and will get there in their own time.

But even these simple agorists may wish to contribute to entrepreneurs specializing in accelerating the movement to the agorist society from statism. And others, perceiving rising inflation heading to economic collapse or gathering clouds of war, will want something done about it. Finally, the counter-attacks of the State which subvert the agorist sub-society and lure libertarians into false paths must be combated. These tasks define the field for the New Libertarian activist. [1]

Again, for those who wish only to live their lives as free as possible and associate with others like-minded, counter-economic libertarianism is sufficient. No more is needed.

But for those who want to support in whatever way they can those heroic entrepreneurs who specialize in recruiting for the agora, deal with State-caused catastrophes, and combat statists within and without, a guide is needed to select those who are "doing something worthwhile" from those spinning their wheels and those actually counter-productive (i.e. counter-revolutionary) to achieving more freedom. And for those like this author, who burn for Liberty and wish to devote themselves to that life's work, a strategy is essential. What follows, then, is the New Libertarian Strategy. [2]

The New Libertarian activist must keep in mind that actual defense against the State is impossible until the counter-economy has generated the syndicates of protection agencies sufficiently large to defend against the remnant of the State. This will occur only at the "phase transition" between the third and fourth steps leading back from our statism to agorism (Chapter 3).

Each step from statism to agorism requires a different strategy; tactics will differ even within each step. There are some rules which will apply in all stages.

Under all circumstances, one recruits and educates. If faced with a confused individual acquaintance that is considering a counter-economic act, encourage them to do it. If they are intelligent enough and not likely to turn on you, explain risks involved and return expected. Most of all, educate them by your example to the extent you can let them know.

All "Library Libertarians" you know those who profess some theoretical variant of libertarianism but eschew practice, should be encouraged to practice what they preach. Scorn their inaction; praise their first halting steps towards counter-economics. Interact with them more and more as trust grows with their competence and experience.

Those already in counter-economics whom you meet can be "let in on" the libertarian philosophy that you hold, that mysterious belief you hold which keeps you so happy and free of guilt. Drop it nonchalantly if they feign lack of interest: wax enthusiastic as they grow more curious and eager to learn.

Engage in self Agorism by example and argument. Control and program your emotional reactions to exhibit hostility at statism and deviationism, and to exhibit enthusiasm and joy at agorist acts and the State's setbacks. Most of these tactics will come with routine but you can check yourself to polish a few things.

Finally, coordinate your activities with other New Libertarian activists. At this point, we arrive at the need for group tactics and organization.

Many worthy libertarians argue that the market structures of businesses, partnerships and joint-stock companies [3] provide all the organization necessary or desirable; save maybe for personal mating or socializing. In one sense they are correct in that all structures must be market-compatible or be inconsistent with agorism. In another sense, they are guilty of a lack of imagination and a concern of form over substance.

In an agorist society, division of labor and self-respect of each worker-capitalist entrepreneur will probably eliminate the traditional business organization – especially the corporate hierarchy, an imitation of the State and not the Market. Most companies will be associations of independent contractors, consultants, and other companies. Many may be just one entrepreneur and all his services, computers, suppliers and customers. This mode of operation is already around and growing in the freer segments of Western economies.

Thus an association of entrepreneurs of liberty for the purpose of specializing, coordinating and delivering libertarian activities is no violation of the market and may well be optimal. The traditional name for a handling together of sovereign units for a goal and then disbanding is an alliance. Hence the basic organization for New Libertarian activists is the New Libertarian Alliance. [4]

The organization of NLA (or NLAs) is simple and should avoid turning into a political organ or even an authoritarian organization. Rather than officers, what are needed are tacticians (local coordinators with competency in tactical planning) and strategists (regional coordinators with competency in strategic thinking). A New Libertarian Ally does not follow a tactician or strategist but rather "buys" their argument and expertise. Anyone offering a better plan can replace the previous planner. Tactics and strategy should be "bought and sold" by the Allies like any other commodity in consistent agorist fashion.

Even though these labels are borrowed from military history and do correspond to a form of combat, never forget that actual physical confrontation with the State's enforcers must await the market's generation of protection agency syndicates of sufficient strength; all else is premature. [5]

What is the global strategy, continental strategy, and local tactics for an NLA to optimally pursue? Again, let's look at the four steps from - or to - agora from Statism. The first three are actually rather artificial divisions; no abrupt change occurs from first to second to third. As will be shown, it is most probable that the transition from the third to fourth step will be quite sudden, though it is not required by the nature of the agora; rather, the convulsion will be caused by the nature of the State. In fact, all violence, unrest, instability and dislocations are caused by the State - never fomented by New Libertarians.

Heed well, you who would be a paladin of Liberty: never initiate any act of violence regardless how likely a "libertarian" result may appear. To do so is to reduce yourself to a statist. There are no exceptions to this rule. Either you are fundamentally consistent or not. A New Libertarian is fundamentally consistent and one who is not fundamentally consistent is not a New Libertarian. [6]

But using New Libertarian analysis, one can predict the likely outbreak of statist aggression and move to head it off by exposure or even defend or evacuate the victims. One can also predict the probable outcomes of deviations by libertarian groups and either head off the sell-outs and disasters or win respect for one's foresight and that of New Libertarianism from potential recruits. Let the State be the forest fire; the NLA are the smoke-eaters who know how it burns, how to firebreak, how the winds of change affect it, where the sparks may fly, and finally, how to extinguish it.

With this in mind, let us label the steps to agora as four phases and outline the appropriate strategy for each.

Phase 0: Zero-Density Agorist Society

In this phase, most of human history, no agorists exist, only scattered libertarians or proto-libertarians thinking and practicing counter-economists. The moment someone reads this manifesto and wishes to apply it, we have moved to the next phase. All that can be done in Phase 0 is slow evolution of consciousness, hit and miss development, and a lot of frustrating dichotomies.

Until you - the first agorist in a Phase 0 situation - have added to your number, your only strategy can be to increase your numbers, as well as live counter-economically yourself. The best form of organization is a Libertarian Alliance in which you steer the members from political activity (where they have blindly gone seeking relief from oppression) and focus on education, publicity, recruitment and perhaps some anti-political campaigning (i.e. "Vote For Nobody," "None of the Above", "Boycott the Ballot," "Don't Vote, It Only

Encourages Them!" etc.) to publicize the libertarian alternative. An LA may take stands on issues agreed on, but insist on unanimity. Only the most clearly libertarian stands will be taken and you can always veto a deviationist stance. Always encourage tendencies towards "hard-core" (consistent) position and scorn "soft-core" (inconsistent) ones.

Phase 1: Low-Density Agorist Society

The first counter-economic libertarians appear in this phase and the first serious splits in the Libertarian movement occur. Since few libertarians are very consistent yet, deviationism will run rife and tend to overwhelm activism. "Get-Liberty-quick" schemes from anarcho-zionism (running away to a Promised Land of Liberty) to political opportunism will seduce the impatient and sway the incompletely informed. All will fail if for no other reason than Liberty grows individual by individual. Mass conversion is impossible. There is one exception - radicalization by statist attack against a collective. Even so, it requires entrepreneurs of Liberty to have sufficiently informed the persecuted collective so that they laze coherently libertarian-ward rather than scatter randomly or worse, flow into out-of-power statism. These Crises of Statism are spontaneous and predictable - but cannot be caused by moral, consistent libertarians.

The strategy of the first New Libertarians is to combat anti-principles which strengthen the State and dissipate anarchist energy uselessly. The general strategy outlines previously applies; get libertarians into counter-economics and get the most active of the agorists to get counter-economists into libertarianism.

The proto-New Libertarians may work within existing organizations and clubs of Libertarians as "radical caucuses," ginger groups, or as a "Libertarian Left" faction in general. An NLA is premature here because it is not yet self-sustaining.

What can be successfully built is - under whatever label seems most conducive for recruitment - a Movement of the Libertarian Left. Such a Movement is itself a mixed bag of individuals of varying "hardness of core" but they are tending or moving towards the ideal of New Libertarianism. Even within MLL structure should be deemphasized. The most New Libertarian will be the most competent to coordinate and plan; that is, those of highest understanding and practice of agorism and greatest zeal for action will naturally direct resources. Each MLLer, like each NL. ally, spends his or her own outsource and decides whether or not to accept a tactician or strategist's advice then planning, as any entrepreneur would do with any informed consultant. Some pseudo-political public trappings may be necessary to utilize public forums and media access; also, most people will not understand your market organization unless you translate it in pseudo-political terminology and back again.

At this point, in the latter stages of Phase 1 and with a functioning MLL large enough, these hard-core dedicated "cadre" can apply leverage to sway larger groups of semi converted quasi-libertarians to actually block marginal actions by the State. This is a high-expenditure, "quick gain," but low long-range yield tactic and should be rare. (It will be covered later; basically, stave off war and mass extermination of libertarians.)

Following all these activities, radicalizing the libertarians, and evolving the NLA. That is all one can accomplish.

Phase 2: Mid-Density, Small Condensation Agorist Society

At this point the statists take notice of agorism. While before libertarians could be manipulated by one ruling faction to the detriment of another (sort of anti-market "competition," played with ballots and bullets rather than innovation and pricing), they will start to be perceived as a a threat. Pogroms (mass arrests) may even occur, although that is unlikely. Remember, most agorists are embedded in the rest of society and associating with them are partially-converted libertarians and counter-economists. In order to reach this phase, the entire society has been contaminated by agorism to a degree. Thus it is now possible for the first "ghettos" or districts of agorists to appear and count on the sympathy of the rest of society to restrain the State from a mass attack. [7]

These communities, whether above or underground, can now sustain the New Libertarian Alliance, NLA acts as spokesman for the agora with the statist society, using every chance to publicize the superiority of agorist living to statist inhabiting and perhaps argue for tolerance of those with "different ways." [8]

In this phase, the agorist society is vulnerable to statist regression of the populace. Thus the agorists, whether visible or not, have a high incentive to at least maintain the present level of libertarian consciousness among the rest of the populace. This being done most expertly by the NLA (one way to define who the NLA is at this phase); the NLA has its sustenance and its mission. But in addition to "defending" the agorist sub-society, it can work towards accelerating the next evolutionary step.

Phase 3: High-Density, Large Condensation, Agorist Society

In this phase, the State moves into a series of terminal crises, somewhat analogous to the well-known Marxist scenario, but with different causes - in this case, real ones. Fortunately, the potential for damage has been drastically decreased by the sapping of the State's resources and corrosion of its authority by the growth of the Counter- Economy.

In fact, as the resources of the economy approach equality between the State and Agora, the State is pushed into crisis. Wars and rampant inflation with depressions and crack-ups become perpetual as the State attempts to redeem its authority. It may be possible to reverse its decline by corrupting the agora with deductive anti-principles, so the NLA's first task is clear: to maintain vigilance and purity of thought. In this phase, the NLA may no longer hold either label or much of its old form. The most motivated New Libertarians will move into the research and development supply for the budding agorist protection and arbitration agencies and lastly as directors of the protection company syndicates.

The situation now approaches revolution but is still reversible. [9] Again the New Libertarians are in the forefront of maintaining and defending gains to this point, but looking ahead to the next phase.

The NLA (now just a collective term for the most forward-looking elements) can accelerate the process by discovering and developing the optimal methods of protection and defense, both by word and deed, for their industry and entrepreneuring its innovations.

At this phase transition between 3 and 4 we have the last unleashing of violence by the Ruling Class of the State to suppress those elements that would bring them to justice for all past state crimes. The State's intellectuals perceive that its authority has failed and all will be lost; things must be reversed now or never. The NLA must prevent premature awareness of this status or premature action on this awareness. This is the final strategic goal of the NLA.

When the State unleashes its final wave of suppression - and is successfully resisted - this is the definition of Revolution. Once realization has occurred that the State no longer can plunder and pay-of its parasitical class, the enforcers will switch sides to those better able to pay them and the State will rapidly implode into a series of pockets of Statism in backward area - if any. [10]

Phase 4: Agorist Society with Statist Impurities

The collapse of the State leaves only mopping up operations. Since the insurance and protection companies see no State to defend against, the syndicate of allied protectors collapses into competition and the NLA - its support gone - dissolves. Statists apprehended pay restoration and if they live long enough to discharge their debts, are re-integrated as productive entrepreneurs (Their "training" comes automatically as they work off their debt.)

We're home (Chapter 2)! New Libertarianism is taken for granted as the basis of ordinary life and we tackle the other problems facing mankind.

Footnotes:

[1] Many agorists such as Pyro Egon have challenged the New Libertarians on this point. As far as they are concerned, the manifesto this far is the entire program and any further "activism" is "movementism" and leads one ineluctably back towards statism.

[2] New Libertarian Strategy is the newsletter of the Movement of the Libertarian Left - not coincidentally.

[3] But not a "corporation" which is a fictitious "individual" created by the State and endowed with privileges. Some privileges besides subsidies and tariffs are special tax rates, limited liability, exemption from regulation, licenses, and legal benefits in court disputes. True, they have some drawbacks but none compares to an unincorporated white-market business.

[4] The first New Libertarian Alliance was formed, prematurely in many respects, by this author in 1974 from recruits from a raid on the "L"P, from other movement activists, and a few counter-economists. The market proved less than ready for a growth in this business and so the NLA to date has spent most of its energies towards building that market.

Any band of New Libertarians can call themselves a New Libertarian Alliances without "official authorization;" most will surely wish to co-ordinate themselves with other NLA groups and try to agree on common strategy, though tactics may differ from different conditions of the Allies.

[5] This mode of NLA organization worked well for the Long Beach chapter that kept it constantly in practice. Regional strategy was not fully "shaken down" by practice but no other NLA group maintained that high a level of committed Allies who were constantly developing and working that theory.

As for armies, it should be noted that Nestor Makhno ran an army in fairly anarchist manner with a small core of officers and complete volunteers filling the ranks when needed or convinced of the need. He fought Reds and Whites successfully in the Ukraine 1918-20 until overwhelmed by weight of numbers of the victorious Red statists combining the full resources of a continent against him.

[6] No membership or credentials is needed or desirable for the NLA. Of course, one may make a list of those with whom to gather and plan, and to whom to mail communications. But there is nothing sacred or special about such lists; they are merely one strategist or tactician's judgment.

One cannot be purged from NLA. One is either a New Libertarian or not according to the evidence provided by one's acts; every other Ally must judge for themselves. All who accept you as a New Libertarian are in Alliance with you; those who reject you are not, though you may be in Alliance with others.

[7] Premature appearance of agorist communities will lead to their suppression violently by the State. The NLA must defend those which can be saved when historical conditions are marginal and warn and evacuate those which are doomed.

[8] It is still within the limits of New Libertarian morality to point out to one faction of the Higher Circles that the agorist existence benefits them ore than the other faction. While no statist can ever be aided in plunder and murder, and even allying with one statist against another consumes scarce resources for the outcome of merely trading oppressors, the New Libertarian can perceive that simply by existing and conducting usual business, the agorist activity is relatively more detrimental to one group of statists over another.

A good rule of thumb to the tactic of playing off ruling groups is to make sure that no more resources are devoted to it than extra statements based in regular publication and media exposure for more important work...and private conversations, if one frequents those social circles.

This tactic fails when the agorist society is perceived as too threatening; then all statist factions unite to save their skins.

[9] Let's say one region is highly agorist and the rest more primitive. Resources may be transferred by the State to crush this premature and localized (thus vulnerable) agora. This applies to Phase 2 even more.

[10] Some will argue that the State may collapse peacefully when the statists see the end approaching. If statists were so reasonable about not resorting to force because of market alternatives, they wouldn't be statists. Revolution is as inevitable as any human action can be.

V. Action! Our Tactics

The previous chapter discussed some tactics in passing. A few that have been found productive for radical libertarians and the MLL include infiltration of less radical groups and sparking splits by presenting alternatives; confrontation of coercion (or deviation) with visible protest and rejection; day to day personal salesmanship among friends; libertarian social groups such as supper clubs to exchange information, goods, and support and act as a proto-agora; and, of course, publication, public speaking, writing fiction with agorist messages [1], and educational activities in many forms: teacher, business consultant, entertainer, revisionist historian, agorist economist, etc.

Successful tactics can only be discovered and used and passed on. Those who perceive sufficiently similar conditions in time and place to those of another where a tactic worked can use it. But it is all a risk; that is what activism is, a type of entrepreneurship, of guessing the market and supplying the demand. One can become better and better at making good guesses; that's what makes a successful entrepreneur. It's all in Human Action by Von Mises if you can apply it.

To find out what has been tried and worked or failed, communication is necessary. If you have reached this page and agreed, and have a desire to support resistance or a burning need to resist coercion, you are ready for the MLL or NLA in existence, depending on the phase we are currently in (Chapter IV). Free yourself. Get active.

What phase are we in? In October 1980 (first edition) most of the planet Earth is in Phase 0. The British Isles, Australia and Canada have moved substantially towards Phase 1; North America is in Phase 1. Only in the highest concentration of libertarians today, in Southern California, are the first signs of Phase 2. Assuming the situation is not reversed, the first few droplets of actual agorist societies - anarchovillages - are nucleating a viable sub-society.

The Movement of the Libertarian Left exists only in California with a few scattered nuclei, agents and cells, in Alliance. The New Libertarian Alliance previously proclaimed was found premature and NLA remains in embryo (or nucleus) until objective conditions arrive to sustain it.

The MLL has its work cut out for it. Externally, the world-wide collapse of the "Left" [2] has weakened restraints on the competitive segments of the State who are rushing towards war to re-mystify their restive victims with patriotism. Seizing the abandoned leadership of the anti-imperialism, anti-war and anti-conscription movement with a fresh, invigorating, ideological backing has become an opportunity for libertarians to become the Left. MLL has to compete with partyarch and monocentrist elements for this pre-eminence. [3]

The lurching of American plutocracy from the brink of runaway inflation to depression and back again, in ever wilder swings, has panicked large numbers of complacent businessmen and raised their consciousness beyond conservative assurances of restoring stability to consider radical and even revolutionary alternatives. Only the Libertarian Left can win these entrepreneurs towards an "ideological," non-pragmatic position. Therein lay our opportunities.

Internally, the "Libertarian" Party has reached a crisis with the 1980 American Presidential election. The premature unmasking of the statism inherent in partyarchy by Crane-Clark's blatant opportunism has managed to generate not only Left opposition but Right and Center opposition. [4] Major defections mount daily. [5]

The failure of some reformist element to oust the Kochtopus by the Denver Convention (August 1981) and lull the unradicalized back in line would set the U.S.L.P. back dramatically and generate thousands of disillusioned recruits for the MLL and anti-party educational and counter-economic activities.

With this manifesto as a manual and inspiration, New Libertarian strategists and tacticians can research, develop, correct and enact the New Libertarian Strategy and the tactics appropriate to the conditions met. Much work is needed but the projects have consequences no mundane work can provide: an end to politics, to taxation, to conscription, to economic catastrophe, to involuntary poverty and to the mass murder of warfare in the final war - society against Our Enemy, The State.

Counter-economics provides immediate gratification for those who abandon statist restraint. Libertarianism rewards the practitioner who follows it with more selfliberation and personal fulfillment than any alternative yet conceived. But only New Libertarianism offers reformation of society into a moral, working way of life without changing the nature of Man. Utopias may be discarded; at last we have a glimpse of how to remold society to fit Man rather than Man to fit some society. What more rewarding challenge could be offered?

Should you now have chosen the New Libertarian path, you may wish to join us in our "Triple A" oath and battle cry, or something like it, and renew yourself with it regularly:

"We witness to the efficacy of freedom and exult in the intricate beauty of complex voluntary exchange. We demand the right of every ego to maximize its value without limit save that of another ego. We proclaim the age of the Market unbound, the natural and proper condition for humanity, wealth in abundance, goals without end or limit, and self-determined meaning for all: Agora.

"We challenge all who would bind us to show us cause; failing proof of our aggression we shatter our fetters. We bring to justice all who have aggressed against any, ever. We restore all who have suffered oppression to their rightful condition. And we destroy forever the Monster of the Ages, the pseudo-legitimized monopoly of coercion, from our minds and from our society, the protector of aggressors and thwarter of justice. That is, we smash the State: Anarchy.

"We exert our wills to our personal limits restrained only by consistent morality. We struggle against anti-principles which would sap our wills and combat all who physically challenge us. We rest not nor waste resource until the State is smashed and humanity has reached its agorist home. Burning with unflagging desire for Justice now and Liberty forever, we win: Action!"

Agora, Anarchy, Action!

Samuel Edward Konkin III

October 12, 1980, Anarchovillage (Long Beach)

Footnotes:

[1] E.g., Alongside Night by J. Neil Schulman (Crown, 1979; Ace, 1982) and expected sequels.

[2] The Left was originally proto-Libertarian, as revisionist historians such as Leonard Liggio point out. In the French Assembly, free marketeer Frederic Bastiat sat next to anarchist Pierre-Joseph Proudhon. Even today Marxists refer to anarchists as "ultraleft" elements. The libertarian and Marxist elements were about equal at the close of the First Workingman's International. The Marxists and their sell-out imitators have been in ascendancy since the 1890's, finally losing belief in themselves with the New Left collapse, the invasion of Czechoslovakia and Afghanistan by the U.S.S.R. and VietNam by China - the "impossible" war between two Marxist States.

[3] Currently, "L"P"R"C and SLS respectively.

[4] The "Right" of current libertarianism is fairly principled but many of the principles hewed to are anti-principles: gradualism, conservatism, reformism and minarchy. Reason magazine and its Frontlines newsletter are its main organs. The "Center" includes Murray Rothbard and his following, now organized in the LP "Radical" Caucus, which supports Clark "critically," i.e., externally, but not internally. The Rothbard Centrists have moved Left by abandoning monocentrism.
[5] Murray Rothbard, as mentioned; the Southern California party Council Director, Dyanne Petersen, others informing this writer of their imminent defection should more "selling-out" occur. It will.

o Special Note to Second Edition: It did

A steady trickle of LP defectors have added to the ranks of MLL month by month since then. At least one new Left Libertarian group, the Voluntaryists, have arisen to compete for the ex-partyarchs. And Murray Rothbard is organizing, at this time, a last-ditch showdown for control of the LP with the Kochtopus remnant at the LP presidential nominating convention to be held in September 1983 in New York City.

AGORIST CLASS THEORY

A Left Libertarian Approach to Class Conflict Analysis

By Wally Conger

Drawing on the unfinished work of Samuel Edward Konkin III

With a foreword by Brad Spangler

DEDICATION

This work is dedicated to Sam, who got the ball rolling.

Foreword

The very term evokes mental imagery, and rightly so, of bloody tyrants and their apologists — from the killing fields of Cambodia to the massacre in the Katyn Forest, from statist dupes calling for more government power to "fight poverty" to Trotsky's bastard ideological grandchildren that are called "neo-conservatives."

It has been a fig leaf for banditry and the ravening twin thirsts for power and blood. It has been the mantra of those who would conspire to realize Orwell's nightmare vision of a totalitarian boot forever stomping on a human face.

I'm referring to the other war — the Class War.

Marxist doctrine held, in a nutshell, that the relationship between the common people (the proletariat) and the elite (capitalists) was a continuation of the master and slave relationship of ancient times — and that any means, regardless of how ostensibly evil it may appear, was justifiable in addressing that iniquitous inequity.

With the meltdown of nearly all avowedly Marxist states in the late 1980s and early 1990s, the notion of a Class Struggle was supposed to be consigned to the dustbin of history along with the rest of the smoke and mirrors of Marxist ideology.

There's only one problem, though — Marx's analysis of the world around him was partly wrong and partly right. Where there is truth, there is relevance. It is time for libertarians to dust off the notions of class struggle, class consciousness, and class warfare in order to place them within an increasingly sophisticated libertarian/anarchist ideological framework under the primacy of the Zero Aggression Principle.

One flaw in Marx's thinking, you see, was his theory of exploitation. Libertarians recognize that there is nothing inherently "exploitative" in any genuinely voluntary agreement, such as agreeing to work for a wage. Likewise, there isn't anything virtuous in subtly coercing compliance with demands for labor to be performed on dictated terms, including wage rates. Where Marx was right in his analysis is that under State Capitalism (as opposed to a truly free market) there is an exploitative relationship between the moneyed interests and the common people. He misidentified the oppressor class, though.

What is this actual oppressor class, you ask? The actual oppressor class is the "political class" as originally identified by the Frenchmen Charles Comte and Dunoyer over 150 years ago. By the "political class" it is meant those who draw their livelihood not from the Market, but from the State. The political class is the parasitic class that acquires its livelihood via the "political means" — through "confiscation, taxation, and other forms of coercion." Their victims are the rest of us — the productive class — those who make their living through peaceful and honest means of any sort, such as a worker or an entrepreneur.

State Capitalism, which most confuse with a free market, is most properly understood as a form of Socialism in a Hayekian sense of statist control. That is to say, it is banditry under guise of law. It would also be economically accurate to label it Fascism, Mercantilism, or Corporate Statism. Conversely, a truly free market (or Capitalism in the Randian sense of non-aggression minus Rand's own personal fetish for Big Business) would, I maintain, bear a striking similarity to the vision of anti-state socialists and distributists.

Wally Conger has distilled in the accompanying text the essence of Samuel Edward Konkin III's unfinished exposition of this class theory, *Agorism Contra Marxism* . I'm deeply honored to present *Agorist Class Theory* .

— *Brad Spangler*

Contents

Introduction

Marxism is dead. This is acknowledged almost everywhere, with the exception of university campuses and among stodgy Old Leftists and uninformed media pundits. "The [Marxist] dream is dead," wrote Samuel Edward Konkin III. "The institutions move on, decadent zombies, requiring dismemberment and burial. The 'gravediggers of capitalism' approach their own internment."

Marxism failed on many fronts, perhaps on all fronts. Most fundamentally, though, its failure was economic. Marx's "map of reality" — his class theory — was fatally flawed, and economics was *the* measure by which his philosophy could be checked with reality. The failure of its economics led inevitably to Marxism's failure to live up to its political and historical predictions. Wrote SEK3:

> "Remember well that Marx outlined history and brooked no significant wandering from the determined course. Should History not unfold according to the *determined* pathway 'scientifically' obtained, *all* Marxist theoretical structure crumbles. ...

> "Marxism failed to produce a 'workable model of reality.' On the other hand, it has won the hearts and souls of billions in the past century. In order to bury Marx, it is necessary to deal with his apparent success, not his failures. His strong points must be overcome, not his weak, if [radical Rothbardians, agorists] hope to replace his vision as the prime inspiration of the Left."

1. The Marxist Appeal

Karl Marx himself asserted that should History fail to bear him out, he would admit he was wrong.

History has passed judgment.

Just as Ludwig von Mises forecast in his landmark book *Socialism* (1922), in which the impossibility of economic calculation under Marxist statism was demonstrated, Marx's economics failed horribly. This economic failure led inevitably to the failure of Marx's political and historical predictions, and Marxist-controlled institutions today coast on intellectual capital and historical inertia.

But Marxism *still* won the hearts and souls of billions in the past century, and continues to do so among many even now. Why? What is Marxism's appeal? Samuel Edward Konkin III wrote:

> "The most appealing part of Marxism may well have been the vision of sociopolitical revolution as a secular apocalypse. While others offered explanations of Revolution, only Marx gave it such meaning. No longer were the oppressed to merely oust the old regime to bring in a new regime brutal in a slightly different way, but *the* Revolution would make things so great that no further revolution was necessary. Marx's legerdemain was actually profoundly conservative; once *the* Revolution was over, there would be no more. Even diehard monarchists flinched from that much stasis.
>
> "Yet the combination was unbeatable to motivate political activists: one all-out effort and then home free. More realistic presentations of Revolution tended to excite less dedication and commitment."

But the truth remains: today, Marxism is bankrupt. On the Left, faith is gone, morale is low, and activism is paralyzed. The Left needs a new ideology to supplant its failed and discredited Marxism. Agorism — the purest, most consistent, and revolutionary form of libertarianism — is that supplanting ideology. Agorism can motivate and direct the underclass's struggle against the overclass — and return the Left to its radical anti-state, anti-war, pro-property, pro-market historical roots. Explained SEK3:

> "Agorism and Marxism agree on the following premise: human society can be divided into at least two classes; one class is characterized by its control of the State and its extraction of unearned wealth from the other class. Furthermore, agorists and Marxists will often point to the same people as members of the overclass and underclass, *especially* agreeing on what each considers the most blatant cases. The differences arise as one moves to the middle of the social pyramid.

> "Agorists and Marxists perceive a class struggle which must continue until a climactic event which will resolve the conflict. Both sides perceive select groups which will lead the victims against their oppressors. The Marxists call these groups of high class consciousness 'vanguards' and then extract even more aware elements designated 'elites of the vanguard.' Agorists perceive a spectrum of consciousness amongst the victims as well, and also perceive the most aware elements as the first recruits for the revolutionary cadre. With the exception of 'intellectuals,' the Marxists and agorists sharply disagree on who these most progressive elements are."

2. Precursors to Marxist Class Theory

Although today's academics largely credit the doctrine of class conflict to Marx and Engels, historian Ralph Raico has for many years advanced the 19th Century classical liberal exploitation theory of Comte and Dunoyer as a much superior, more correct precursor to the Marxist class model. However, Konkin begins his examination of class theories much earlier than Comte-Dunoyer or Marx. He wrote:

> "Rome had three citizen classes and a fourth alien class written into its legal codes. Medieval Europe continued the concepts and much of the rest of the world had its versions. The upper class was the nobility, that is, the royalty and aristocracy, who controlled the land and directed its resources. The lower classes were those who worked that land, peasants, serfs, villeins, *etc.* Most people fit in the lower class but those that fit in neither were, at least in numbers, at least as numerous as the upper class. Many were merchants, and as they turned villages into towns and then large, powerful cities, they were given the term Middle Class or terms meaning city-dweller: burger, bourgeois, *etc.*"

Enter Comte, Dunoyer, and the rest of the "French school." But we will get to libertarian (and agorist) class theory later.

First...Karl Marx.

3. Marxist Classes

Marx recognized that the millennium-old class structure of Europe was drastically and noticeably changing and that he lived in a revolutionary time. As SEK3 explained:

> "The old order was making way for a new one. The Aristocracy was on its way out, either to liquidation (as in France and the U.S.) or to vestigial status, kept around for ceremonial purpose by a sentimental bourgeoisie (and lower classes) as in England. The bourgeoisie was in the ascendancy in the first half of the nineteenth century — Marx's formative and most active years.

> "Future events could and were explained by this class struggle theory: the Europe-wide rebellion of 1848 swept away much of aristocratic power restored after Napoleon's defeat; the American Civil War was the Northern bourgeoisie's way of smashing the remnant of landed aristocracy preserved as by the South.

> "While this phenomenon *so far* was widely acknowledged (though it applied poorly to the Franco-Prussian War of 1870-1), Marx was as interested in the transformation of the *Lower* Class as in that of the Upper Class. Peasants were being driven off their farms, serfs were given their freedom to go to the cities to become industrial workers. And here was the focus of Marx's insight."

First, based on Adam Smith's Labor Theory of Value, Marx saw the evolving workers as the only real productive class. He saw the bourgeoisie evolving into a smaller, aristocratic group that held ownership of the new means of production: factories, assembly lines, distribution/ transportation systems, etc. The world, Marx said, was being neatly divided between a non-productive class (the former bourgeoisie, now *capitalists)* and a productive class skilled in using capital goods but not owning them (the *proletariat*). Capital would control the State. To Marx, this was the world of the future, as evident in his present.

Marx's second insight was based on Hegel's dialectical materialism. History was an ongoing clash of ideas: the thesis existed, the anti-thesis rose in opposition, and the clash created a synthesis (a new thesis). Wrote SEK3: "This is why Marxist sloganeers always call for 'struggle' — it's all their theory allows them to do!"

So just as the bourgeoisie ousted the aristocracy to create capitalism (the synthesis), Marx declared that the new proletariat would oust capital and synthesize into, well, nothing. The proletariat victory, Marx predicted, would eventually end classes and class conflict. Granted, the proletariat (or, rather, its vanguard elite) would control the State temporarily. But once classes vanished and there was no class conflict to repress, the State would "wither away."

4. The Agorist Critique of Marxist Class Theory

Marx's Class Theory failed to see that those workers classically considered proletariat would become growingly obsolescent. In North America, unionized skilled workers are in *decline,* being absorbed by new entrepreneurship (franchising, independent contracting and consulting), the service industry, scientific research and development, increased managerial function *without* human labor underneath for exploitation, and bureaucracy. Wrote SEK3:

> "The entrepreneurial problem is unsolvable for Marxism, because Marx failed to recognize the economic category. The best Marxists can do is lump them with new, perhaps mutated, capitalist forms. But if they are to fit the old class system, they are *petit bourgeois,* the very group that is to either collapse into proletarians or rise into the monopoly capitalist category. Small business should *not* increase in the 'advanced, decadent stages of capitalism.' "

Marxism also does not deal with the persistent Counter-Economy (i.e., a peaceful black market or underground economy). There is a spectrum of the Counter-Economy "tainting" workers, entrepreneurs, and even capitalists. Said Konkin:

> "Scientists, managers, even civil servants do not merely accept bribes and favors but actively seek second, unreported employment in the 'black market.' And the more 'socialist' the State, the bigger the *nalevo,* 'black work' or 'underground' component of the economy.... [T]his turns Marx 'on his head' ...: 'advanced capitalism' is generating runaway free-enterprise (the Old-Fashioned kind) in reaction; the more decadent (statist) the capitalism, the more virulent the reaction and the larger the Counter-Economy.

> "But even worse is the class of Counter-Economists. That is, by Marxist class structure, the black marketeers cannot *be* a class: workers, capitalists and entrepreneurs in active collusion against a common enemy, the State. True, many do not perceive themselves as in a common class and some even try to deny their 'black' activities even

to themselves, thanks to religious and social guilt induction. And yet, when the agents of the State appear to enforce the 'laws' of the Power Elite, the Counter-Economists from tax dodging businessman to drug-dealing hippie to illegal alien to feminist midwife are willing to signal each other with the universal: 'Watch it, the fuzz/pigs/ *flics / federales / etc. !'* ...

"Even in extreme cases, the commonality of the Counter- Economist has generated an economic determinism as strong as any Marx considered to weld 'class unity.' But this is *still* not the worst.

"This class unity is not that of a workers' class (though workers are heavily involved) nor of a capitalist class (though capitalists are involved) nor even of a ruling class — this class is based on the commonality of *risk,* arising from a common source (the State). And risk is *not* proletarian (or particularly capitalist); it is *purely entrepreneurial.*

"Again, to make it clear, if the 'entrepreneuriat' are tossed into the capitalist class, then the Marxist must face the contradiction of 'capitalists' at war with the capitalist-controlled State.

"At this point, Marx's class analysis is in shreds. Clearly, oppression exists, but another model is needed to explain how it works."

5. Libertarian Class Analysis

Marx's class analysis, with its recurring problem of the cross-class nature of statists and anti-statists, lies in shreds. Clearly, oppression exists, but another class model is needed to explain how it works.

The Libertarian Class Model advanced by Murray N. Rothbard is based on the relation of the individual to the State, which springs from Franz Oppenheimer's paradigm of the evolution of the State. The sweep of history, Oppenheimer wrote, was a long account of the parasitic class continually transforming itself with new religions and ideologies to justify its existence and repeatedly hoodwink the productive class into serving it. As SEK3 explained:

> "Today the State uses democracy (victim participation in his own plunder), liberalism (leash the State to make it more palatable), conservatism (unleash the State against 'enemies' — commies or capitalists, perverts or straights, heretics or orthodox believers, difference 1 or difference 2), and other nostrums, snake-oil or anticoncepts to beguile its victims into accepting continued plunder (taxation), murder (war and execution), and slavery (conscription and taxation again)."

Socialism, including Marxist variants, is just another dogma used to justify the State's existence, and it is one of the most appealing.

Almost all libertarians accept that the State divides society into two classes: those who gain by the existence of the State and those who lose. Most libertarians also agree that society would be better off if the State were eliminated or at least shrunk significantly. But despite efforts of the late Rothbard and others to raise libertarian class consciousness, most American libertarians seem to find discussion of class theory offensive, "impolite," and "not respectable." They appear to believe that only rightwing kooks and commies talk about ruling classes and class structures. Nevertheless, efforts to expand Libertarian Class Theory into a comprehensive model have continued.

6. Radical Libertarian Class Analysis

Murray Rothbard himself continued to expand upon Libertarian Class Theory. His roots in the Old Right had introduced him to populist "bankers conspiracy" theories and the like. Added class viewpoints came from Left-statists and earlier anarchists. What he discovered was that the proponents of ruling classes, power elites, politico-economic conspiracies, and Higher Circles pointed to roughly the same gang at the top of the sociological pyramid.

Rothbard introduced the work of three Left Revisionist analysts to Libertarian Class Theory: Gabriel Kolko, Carl Oglesby, and G. William Domhoff.

Historian Kolko's *Triumph of Conservatism* detailed how "capitalists" thwarted the relatively free marketplace of the late 19th century and conspired with the State to become "robber barons" and monopolists. Rothbard's adoption of the Kolko viewpoint severed the alliance between radical libertarians and free-market apologists for conservatism.

Oglesby, a former president of Students for a Democratic Society, coauthored *Containment and Change* in 1967, which argued for an alliance between the New Left and the libertarian, non-interventionist Old Right in opposing imperialistic U.S. foreign policy. In *The Yankee and Cowboy War* (1976), Oglesby tied in current assassination-conspiracy theories to present a division in the ruling class. Important for both Rothbard and Oglesby was the division within the Higher Circles; the internal conflict between those controlling the State manifests itself in political electioneering, corruption and entrapment (Watergate), assassination and, finally, outright warfare. Wrote SEK3: "The class consciousness of the super-statists, while high, does not include class solidarity."

What were the "Higher Circles"? The term came from Domhoff, a research professor of psychology, who described them as a subtle aristocracy with similar mating habits and association characteristics previously seen in other holders of State power and privilege. Rothbard's discovery and dissemination of Domhoff's work provided a solid base for his Power Elite analysis.

In nearly every ruling-class theory, the top of the statist pyramid was occupied by David Rockefeller's interlocking-directorate corporate control of U.S. and international finance and the band of Court Intellectuals and corporate allies found in the Council on Foreign Relations, the Trilateral Commission, and lesser-known groups. Once a ruling group was identified, its nature could be examined further and its actions observed and eventually predicted.

Two formidable blocks have prevented even the *radical* libertarians from offering a *comprehensive* class model to compete with essentially dead Marxist alternatives. The first block is a "culture lag," most notably in the U.S., where talking about classes is perceived as "offensive" and "impolite." As SEK3 remarked, "Only rightist kooks and commies talk about ruling classes and class structures."

The second roadblock is simply the limitation of libertarian theory. With the exception of agorists, even most radical libertarians see a political solution to statism. Wrote Konkin:

> "In building political coalitions to seize the apex of State control, it pays not to look too closely at the class interests of your backers and temporary allies. ...

> "This limitation can be understood in another way. When libertarian ideologues attack alleged libertarians for not freeing themselves of State institutions, State subsidies, or actual State jobs, they reply *'tu quoque.'* That is, how can the 'purist' libertarians enjoy the supposed benefits of State roads, monopolized postal delivery and even municipal sidewalks and then accuse those wearing a Libertarian label of selling out by getting elected to office, accepting tax-collected salaries and wielding actual political power — on the way to 'withering away' the State, no doubt.

> "Agorists have had no such problem with a distinction, nor do they find any disjunction between means and ends. Furthermore, the simple premises of agorist class theory lead quickly to sharp judgments about the moral nature (in libertarian theory) and practical nature of any

individual's human action. That is, agorists have a comprehensive class theory ready to supplant the Marxist paradigm which also avoids the flaws in semi-libertarian halfhearted theory and its attendant compromises. As to be expected, it begins with Counter-Economics."

7. Agorist Class Theory

Murray Rothbard took Franz Oppenheimer's distinction between the political means of gaining wealth (State theft) and the economic means (production) and then portrayed them as Power vs. Market (in his book *Power and Market*). Unfortunately, most libertarians haven't applied Rothbard's concept completely and thoroughly. Explained Konkin:

> "Since many libertarians arrived at anarchy from the limited government, classical liberal position, they retain a sort of three-cornered concept of struggle: the State at one apex, 'real' criminals at a second, and innocent society at a third. Those who commit victimless crimes, in the minarchist view, may often be put in the criminal class not for their non-crime victimless act but for avoiding trial by the State and remaining at large. Again, some anarchists have yet to entirely free themselves from this liberal statist hangover.

> "Remember, the liberal statists want to restrain the State to increase the production of the host to maximize eventual parasitism. They 'control their appetites' but continue the system of plunder. The recent political example of supply-side economics starkly illustrates the basic statist nature of such ideas: the tax rate is lowered in order to encourage greater economic production and thus a greater total tax collection in the long run."

Likewise, "free-enterprise" conservatives, and "libertarian" minarchists call for retention of the State, however restricted or restrained. They are the *enemy* of the agorists, the free market, and complete liberty. They fall on the statist side of the class line. "The libertarian rhetoric they offer," Konkin wrote, "may be 'turned' or continued to consistency in winning over confused and marginal potential converts — but they offer no material substance for freedom. That is, they are *objectively statists*."

What is meant when a person or group or people are called *objectively statist?* To agorists, the term is used for those who emulate the State by murdering, stealing, defrauding, raping, and assaulting. "These 'red marketeers' (dealing in blood, not gold or trade goods)," SEK3 explained, "are best looked upon as degenerate factions of the ruling class, in contention with the State's police as the Cowboys fight the Yankees, the Morgans fight the Rothchilds or the Rockefellers, and the Soviet statists fight the American statists." These "red marketeers," say agorists, are *criminals.*

At the same time, all so-called (by the State) "criminals" (or criminal acts) that do not involve initiation of violence or the threat of it (coercion) are counter-economic. Since they run counter to the interests (real or perceived) of the State, and are usually *productive,* they are forbidden by the State. They are, therefore, *objectively agorist* and thus *objectively revolutionary.* Wrote Konkin:

> "Agorist class theory has the best of both positions: a sharp class line *and* a graduated spectrum. Individuals are complex and confused. An individual may commit some Counter-Economic acts and some statist ones; nonetheless, each act is either Counter-Economic or statist. People (and groups of people) can be classified along a spectrum as to the predominance of agorism over statism. Yet at each given moment, one can view an action, judge it immediately, and take concrete counter-action or supportive action, if desired."

What about motivation, awareness, consciousness of actions and their consequences, and professions of agreement? They are irrelevant; agorists judge one solely by one's acts. And one is responsible for fully restoring one's victims to the pre-aggression state of being for each and every act (see *New Libertarian Manifesto* , chapter 2). Konkin explains:

> "Regular, repeated patterns of aggression make one a habitual criminal — a statist (or 'pure statist'). These people earn no wealth and have no property. Their loot is forfeit to revolutionary agorists as agents of the victims. The pure statist subclass includes all political officeholders, police, military, civil service, grant holders and subsidy receivers. There is a special subclass of the pure statists who not only accept plunder and enforce or maintain the machinery of the State but actually direct and control it. In 'socialist' countries, these are the top officeholders of the governing political party who usually (though not always) have top government offices. In the 'capitalist' countries, these super-statists seldom appear in government positions, preferring to control directly the wealth of their state-interfaced corporations, usually banks, energy monopolists and army suppliers. Here we find the Power

Elite, Higher Circles, Invisible Government, Ruling Class and Insider Conspiracy that other ideological groupings have detected and identified.

"Towards the other end of the spectrum [from statists] are fulltime counter-economists," SEK3 explained. "They reject government offerings and disregard State regulations. If they report an income, it is a tiny proportion of what they actually earn; if they file a report, it's highly misleading but plausible. Their occupations are fulfilling demand that the State strives to suppress or exterminate. They not only act freely, but often heroically."

Just as the super-statists understand the State's workings and use it consciously, there exist those at the counter-economic end of the spectrum who understand the pure libertarian consistency and morality of their acts; these are the agorists. "Against the Power Elite is the anti-power elite — the Revolutionary Agorist Cadre (or New Libertarian Alliance)," Konkin wrote.

But what of the "middle class" on the spectrum? What of those who mix commission of *some* counter-economic acts (black spots) with *some* statist acts (white spots), their lives summed up by grayness? Konkin described the middle-class this way:

> "To the statists, they are the victims, the herds of cattle to be slaughtered and sheep to be sheared. To the Agorists, they are the external marketplace, to receive nearly everything in trade — but trust.
>
> "And some day they shall either take control of their lives and polarize one way or the other, or fail to do so and shall stagnate in the statist swamp or be borne away on the winds of revolutionary change."

Konkin offered a scenario, using agorist class theory, to illustrate the difference between a limited-government libertarian and an agorist:

> "Consider the individual standing at the corner of the street. He can see two sides of the building behind him as he prepares to cross the street. He is hailed and turns around to see an acquaintance from the local libertarian club approaching in one direction. The latter advocates 'working through the system' and is an armed government agent. Walking along the other side of the building is another acquaintance, same age, gender, degree of closeness and so on, who is a practicing counter-economist. She also may be armed and is undoubtedly carrying

the very kind of contraband the State's agent is empowered to act on. Seeing you, the first individual waves and confirms she indeed has the illegal product — and is about to run into the 'libertarian statist' at the corner. Both are slightly distracted, looking at you.

"The situation is not likely to happen too often but it's quite possible. Only the removal of 'complicating factors' is contrived. If you fail to act, the counter-economist will be taken by surprise and arrested or killed. If she is warned, she may — at this last-minute — elect to defend herself before flight and thus injure the agent. You are aware of this and must act now — or fail to act.

"The agorist may take some pains to cover his warning so that he will not get involved in a crossfire, but he will act. The socialist has a problem if the State agent works for a socialist state. Even the 'libertarian' has a problem. Let's make it really rough: the State agent contributes heavily to the local 'libertarian' club or party (for whatever reasons; many such people are known to this author). The counter-economist refuses to participate except socially to the group. For whose benefit would the 'political libertarian' act?
"Such choices will increase in frequency when the State increases repression or the agorists increase their resistance. *Both* are likely in the near future.

"Agorist class theory is quite practical."

8. Agorist Solutions for Marxist Problems

Marxist Problem: The revolutionary class appears to work against its own interest; the proletariat support reactionary politicians.

Agorist Solution: The Counter-Economic class *cannot* work against its interests as long as it is acting counter-economically. Those supporting statists politically have internal psychological problems without doubt, but as a class, these acts dampen the weakening of the State marginally. (Someone who earns $60,000 tax-free and contributes up to $3000 politically is a net revolutionary by several thousand dollars, several hundred percent!)

———

Marxist Problem: "Revolutionary" States keep "selling out" to reaction.

Agorist Solution: There are no such states. Resistance to *all* states at all times is supported.

———

Marxist Problem: Revolutionary parties often betray the victimized class before taking power.

Agorist Solution: There are no such parties; resistance to *all* parties at all times is supported.

———

Marxist Problem: Little objective relief can be accomplished by reformist action. (Agorists *agree!)* Therefore, one must await the revolution to destroy the system. Until then, revolutionary activities are premature and "adventurist." Still, the productive class remains victimized until the class reaches consciousness *as a whole.*

Agorist Solution: Each individual may liberate himself immediately. Incentives for supporting collective action are built in and grow as the self-conscious counter-economy (agora) grows.

———

Marxist Problem: The class line blurs with time — against prediction.

Agorist Solution: Class lines sharpen with time — as predicted.

Appendix

***Cui Bono?* Introduction to Libertarian Class Theory (1973)**

By Samuel Edward Konkin III

Libertarianism has been denounced by William F. Buckley as "extreme apriorism" (in reference to Murray N. Rothbard in "Notes Toward an Empirical Definition of Conservatism"). Indeed, Libertarians can willingly concede the substance of the charge, if not the pejorative implication of heresy. The fundamental libertarian premise of non-aggression — of unbending opposition to all forms of initiatory violence and coercion to life and property — gives the libertarian analyzing his societal context and seeking out ways of dealing with it a logical "razor" of exceptional keenness. With it, he can slash away the fat of special pleading of various ideologies and retain the lean meat of genuine contributions to his understanding. Perhaps no other ideology, not even Marxism, has such a quality of over-all integration and self-consistency, as indicated by the startling rapidity that this new and complex theory is transmitted to new libertarians.

What follows is an excellent example of the use of "Rothbard's Razor" in synthesizing an approach and understanding in an area almost devoid of libertarian sources.

The author readily acknowledges that his only original contribution to this field is one of collation and organization of scattered writings absorbed during his intellectual maturation which was fortunate enough to coincide with that of Libertarianism. Above all, acknowledgement is accorded to *The Libertarian Forum,* Dr. Murray N. Rothbard, and the scholars he inspired.

I. Economic Analysis of Libertarian Class Theory

Dr. Rothbard has noted the inspiration he gained from John C. Calhoun that the State — which we recognize as the monopoly of legitimized coercion — divides men into two classes. The State's systematic looting of the general public and subsequent distribution of this wealth necessarily distorts the allocation of property that would exist in a free market. By a free market, libertarians mean one in which all goods and services are voluntarily exchanged. An analysis of involuntary exchanges is provided by *Power and Market* by Dr. Rothbard. At the very least, the resources consumed by the individuals who make up the State's bureaucracy constitute a net gain by these wielders of power (or they would not engage in the practice) and constitute a net loss to their victims even if the remains were distributed as equitably as possible. In practice, far more is consumed by the Statists and their chosen beneficiaries and is lost by the victims. This is the fundamental division observed by Calhoun and Rothbard: the division of society into an exploiting class of those who make a net gain by the existence of the State, and an exploited class of those who incur a net loss by the existence of the State.

The charge immediately arises that nearly everybody in the modern complex mixed economy makes gains and losses from the State's actions. Separation and accounting is extraordinarily difficult. Libertarians must agree but respond that firstly, one can improve the moral character of one's own life by striving to comprehend his sources of wealth, maximizing the non-coercive ones and minimizing the coercive ones, and, secondly, that those enjoying or suffering an extreme imbalance can be discerned and dealt with. Those who are obviously suffering heavy oppression deserve the priority attention from those libertarian humanists concerned with aiding and relieving victims of the State. Those who are obviously gaining overwhelmingly by the State (the "Ruling Class") can be rightly suspected of directing State policy and becoming priority targets of those libertarian activists interested in achieving a just society.

II. Historical Analysis of Libertarian Class Theory

Here Dr. Rothbard has drawn heavily upon the studies of the German sociologist Franz Oppenheimer (The *State)* and his American disciple, Albert Jay Nock (Our *Enemy, the State)*. Oppenheimer distinguished two means of acquiring wealth — the economic means and the political means. These correspond to wealth acquired voluntarily by the market and to wealth acquired coercively by power.

I have been fond of using the following paradigm to synopsize Oppenheimer's thesis. Peaceful farmers and agorists (*agora* = open marketplace) are engaged in production and trade, having judges, perhaps priests, and chiefs who organize defense against predatory tribes and roving bands of thieves. These bands of savages raid such productive communities for their own parasitical gain, taking all removable wealth, including slaves, and consuming fixed wealth through fire, rape, and murder. Even if constantly successful, the leaders of these raiders soon realize that they will eventually run out of sources of wealth. The first step toward civilization is then taken by leaving behind enough wealth and populace to rebuild so that they may be raided again. The parasites cease to be fatal to their hosts. Of course, the threat of an annual raid during harvest, for example, is somewhat discouraging to the incentive of the productive victims. The more enlightened barbarians move on to the next step — occupying the agorist communities, institutionalizing and regularizing the plunder and rape (e.g., taxation, *droit de seigneur)*. These rulers seek to counter discouragement, resentment, and rebellion by allying (or buying out) the Priests to exalt the ruling class and to convince victims that they are actually benefiting by the presences of these "protectors of order." Later in history, this function of creating a mind-numbing mystique is taken up by Court Intellectuals as religion wanes.

The plunderers can arise internally, too. Perhaps the War Chiefs and native Priests, seeing the examples around them, convince the locals that they too need a strong standing force to defend the community against invasion by the foreign States. Creating the same mystique, the protectors become the plunderers and a new State is born.

Oppenheimer's theory complements the Calhoun - Rothbard analysis perfectly by explaining the origins of the present-day States. For a study of actual modern nation-states and the operation of their class structures, we turn to the Revisionist Historians.

III. Revisionist Contributions to Libertarian Class Theory

World War I ruptured the liberal and radical intellectual body. Even anarchists divided on the War Question. The anti-war group among historians began delving into the records to prove the correctness of their opposition and demonstrate to the more idealistic War supporters how they were duped into serving plutocratic war "profiteers," political chicanery, and closet Imperialism. The widespread disillusionment with the Treaty of Versailles aided such Revisionists and won general acceptance to their exposures. Charles Beard, Harry Elmer Barnes, Sidney Fay, J.W. Pain, and W.L. Langer in the U.S.; J.S. Ewart in Canada; Morel, Beazley, Dickinson, and Gooch in England; Fabré-Luce. Renouvin, and Demartial in France; Stieve, Montgelas, von Wegerer, and Lutz in Germany; and Barbagallo, Torre, and Lumbroso in Italy: these historians became quite chic, especially as leaders arose in the defeated powers to revise the terms of the Treaty, and "appeasers" in the victorious powers to accommodate them.

World War II caused a new split, with Beard, Barnes, Charles C. Tansill in the U.S., and F.J.P. Veale and A.J.P. Taylor remaining (or becoming) Revisionist on the Second War, with others going a-whoring after the new War to End All Wars. This time, the victorious powers managed to impose a "Historical Blackout" through the extensive Court Intellectuals influence in ever more State-financed Universities and historical journals on the Revisionists. The courageous dissenters were vilified as thinly-disguised Nazi-symps, though many had impeccable liberal and social-democratic credentials. Pacific Front revisionism has had some measure of success, but European Front revisionism remains a disreputable activity.

Cold War Revisionism is accepted somewhat less than WWI but more than WWII inquiry and exposure. Most encouragingly, the New Left and "deviationist Marxist" historians who were drawn into Revisionism by their antipathy to the Vietnam War have begun looking backwards for the roots of modern foreign policy.

On the Left, Weinstein and Gabriel Kolko have integrated Revisionist History on foreign policy with domestic ruling class investigation. On the Right, the Birchers have grown gradually less hysterical in their "Conspiracy Theory," dropping their International Communist deviltheory for exposure of the machinations of U.S. plutocrats.

The Higher Circles by G. William Domhoff begins the synthesis of the varying strands of revisionism into a single sober thesis, adding the sociological surveys of C. Wright Mills "Power Elite" investigations. Domhoff, a Leftist, devotes a section of his book to an earlier rightist conspiracy theorist, Dan Smoot, and finds much of it agreeable. Since then, Smoot has been superseded by Gary Allen's *None Dare Call It Conspiracy.*

IV. Libertarian Class Theory — Application to Domestic Policy

Beard goes back to the American secession from the British Empire with his *Economic Interpretation of the Constitution.* Libertarians tend to begin with the relatively laissez-faire period of the late Nineteenth Century in the U.S., explored by Kolko in his magnificent *Triumph of Conservatism.* Kolko deviates from orthodox Marxism by claiming that the wicked capitalists did not establish their rule due to inevitable concentration of economic power under capitalism, but rather plotted to gain the State's aid in destroying an all-too-successful competitive semi-free market which threatened the long-term stability of their profits.

Kolko devastatingly points out that the massive regulations of transportation and anti-trust legislation advocated by the anti-monopolistic Progressive movement was actively supported by such powerful businessmen as Andrew Carnegie, Mellon, Morgan, and Rockefeller. In 1905, the National Civics Federation was formed to combat the "anarchist" tendencies of the laissez-faire oriented National Association of Manufacturers (mostly small businessmen with little vested interest wanting to grow, not stand pat). NCF members were urged to support regulations and labor legislation to integrate the labor aristocracy as junior partners in the emerging new ruling class. Over the years, the Higher Circles developed the Council on Foreign Relations to influence U.S. State Foreign Policy (tied internationally to similar groups in Western Europe through the "Bilderbergers") and the Committee for Economic Development for U.S. State Domestic Policy.

Recently, Ralph Nader has been astonished by the discovery that most of the Regulatory Boards are run by the very industries they were set up to control. One can only begin to imagine what the CFR-CED crowd is doing with the Wage-Price Controls. The CLIC claque is made up of equal representation of Big Business, Big Labor, and Government. Surprise, surprise.

V. Libertarian Class Theory — Application to Foreign Policy

The financing of World War I has some incredible anecdotes associated with it. For example, there were the Warburg Brothers, one financing the German War Effort, the other the Allied Effort. There were bauxite mines in France which provided aluminum for German War Planes, and the activities of the "Merchants of Death," munitions manufacturers selling to all sides, would be comic if the millions of deaths could be dissociated.

Modern revisionist theory begins with the attempts of the Bank of England to restore the pound's value. The massive inflation of the War made it impossible to restore it to its pre-war value in gold, and exacting reparations from Germany led to a hyperinflation and crack-up boom smashing the German economy (and led to the 1923 Putsch). The Bank's Ashley Montagu met with American financiers in Georgia for the purpose of depreciating U.S. currency to improve the relative standing of the pound. Already, the British were clubbing their East European satellites (created between the USSR and Germany by that perfidious Treaty) into following their economic policy.

The Federal Reserve Board's inflation of the Roaring Twenties (a boom fueled by that very same monetary expansion) led to the Crash, Depression, and Roosevelt's fascist NRA and IRS jackbooters raiding homes to seize the recently outlawed metal, gold. And, of course, the European fascist autarchies, ripped loose from the world plutocrats' control, engaged in barter competition with their own interest in mind, and brought on the Second World War in retaliation.

This time, the American Military-Industrial Complex was *not* dismantled. (See James J. Martin's *Revisionist Viewpoints* for a truly horrifying speech reprinted which was given in 1940 advocating just that and telling businessmen to get with it — "it" being the coming new world order.) A new International Threat to Peace was needed, and less than two years after the end of the Second War to End All Wars, Churchill announced that "an Iron Curtain has fallen across Europe."

Considerable investigation of plutocratic beneficiaries of the Vietnam War is underway, much less so of those benefiting from the Middle East conflict. Some libertarians have already begun to project the interests of the exploiting class power elite to predict the next War.

VI. Alternative Interpretations

A. Marx

While Marxist historical economic determinism draws many scholars in that camp to similar conclusions as those of libertarians, it contains several fatal flaws — over and above the obvious one of economic misunderstanding. The necessity for rigid adherence to a class struggle interpretation based on wealth possession rather than on the means of its acquisition and to an inevitable coming of a proletariat revolution led by organized labor forces the Marxist to judge and rationalize his conclusions to fit at all costs. Perhaps just as devastatingly, Marxism is now a "religion" justifying the existence of dozens of the States in the world, and Marxists are now playing Court Intellectuals and suppressing Revisionists in their midst.

B. Consensus

The "consensus" school, the dominant group of Court Historians in the West, deny the existence of any classes. While there may have been wicked exploiters in the past, they were routed and brought to justice by the Progressive Era, the New Deal, the Fair Deal, the New Frontier, and the Great Society, and whatever is to come. We are left to assume that all these plutocrats are receiving windfalls by the failure of previous reformers to spot all the loopholes and economic imperfections in the free market.

And if the plutocrats who gained the most from State intervention supported Roosevelt, Wilson, Roosevelt, Truman, Kennedy, Johnson, and whoever succeeds Nixon...must be a lot of accidents, coincidences, and the inability of these people to perceive their own real interests but lucking out anyways?

C. Rand

No one would accuse Ayn Rand of being a competent historian or leader of a school of historiography. Unfortunately, she does convey an implicit interpretation of history which lingers in many of those deserting Objectivism for Libertarianism. In her view, similar to the Consensus school but inverted in moral judgment, peaceful productive capitalists were engaged in making everyone well off in the Nineteenth Century, when along came these Progressive collectivists drunk on Statism and high on altruism, to ravish their profits and lay their clammy hands on their activities (strictly between consenting adults). Having absorbed too much altruist collectivism themselves, the capitalists gave up the intellectual battle for their freedom and tried to pragmatically accommodate themselves to the new system, leading them to supporting pragmatist thugs like Nixon's "plumbers."

While I certainly would not disagree with the need to straighten out a lot of businessmen philosophically and ethically, Rand's ignoring (and/or ignorance) of the powerful with vested interest in the State leaves the Objectivist with the tactics of parlor debates and pamphleteering as his only defense against the guns and prisons of the Statists. What frustration the Objectivist must feel hearing that Richard Nixon has read *Atlas Shrugged* and still has not seen the light! If only David Rockefeller would just listen to him for a minute...

VII. Value of Libertarian Class Theory

Several good reasons have already been suggested in this article for the study and application of libertarian class theory. Understanding the nature of the enemy never hurts in dealing with him. Turning over the Rank of Vested Interest on an issue to expose the Plutocratic worms crawling out from under may turn public pressure on to force the power elite to accommodate the dissent and give up untenable activities. Convincing New Leftists and Birchers that you are, indeed, aware of the problem and you can explain the Ruling Class/Conspiracy even better should aid in recruiting. Fingering the Court Intellectuals as tools of the interests they were supposed to forsake in their supposed search for Truth and Enlightenment could shake-up a few academies and compromise the credibility of these modern Witch-Doctors purveying their sophisticated voodoo.

Murray Rothbard urges the libertarian activist to burn with a passion for justice. If this is our Quest, then Libertarian Class Theory is indispensable to the discovery of those who have visited statism upon us, and whose blood-drenched hands are pocketing the booty.

Old fashioned justice is needed for a new liberty.

[This article first appeared in *New Libertarian Notes* #28, December 1973.]

www.ingramcontent.com/pod-product-compliance
Lightning Source LLC
Chambersburg PA
CBHW031145250726
48655CB00002B/846